D0870137

Contents

WHAT IF
PARENTING
IS THE *Most*
Important
JOB IN THE WORLD?

SANDY CALWELL

20 *Lessons You
Want to Teach
Your Own Children*

FERNE PRESS

What If Parenting is the Most Important Job in the World?
20 Lessons You Want to Teach Your Own Children
Copyright © 2011 by Sandy Calwell
Printed in Canada

Summary: Author Sandy Calwell loved her life as a successful career woman—until she gave birth to her son Kasey and fell in love with motherhood. *What If Parenting is the Most Important Job in the World?* describes, in detail, the reasons Sandy decided to quit her job and become a full-time parent.

Library of Congress Cataloging-in-Publication Data
Calwell, Sandy
What If Parenting is the Most Important Job in the World? 20 Lessons You Want to Teach Your Own Children/Sandy Calwell-First Edition/
Sandy Calwell– First Edition
ISBN-13: 978-1-933916-58-3
ISBN-10: 1-933916-53

1. Family and Relationships. 2. Parenting. 3. Faith. 4. Motherhood.
5. Career Transition.
I. Calwell, Sandy II.What If Parenting is the Most Important Job in the World?
20 Lessons You Want to Teach Your Own Children
Library of Congress Control Number: 2010940180

Manufactured by Friesens Corporation
in Altona, Manitoba, January 2011
Docket 62532

FERNE PRESS

Ferne Press is an imprint of Nelson Publishing & Marketing
366 Welch Road, Northville, MI 48167
www.nelsonpublishingandmarketing.com
(248) 735-0418

Preface

"The time is always right to do what is right."
~ Martin Luther King, Jr.

It is said that the biggest journey is started with the smallest step. If that's the case, my life so far has been the culmination of hundreds of little steps: steps that became small incremental decisions leading me toward goals I initially would have never imagined. Years ago, I made the decision to jump off the traditional work track and step into a more personally oriented life that focused on my family.

The physical act of climbing a ladder takes trust. When we climb one, we are placing trust in the construction and physical condition of the frame, the stability of the steps, and the safety of the location where it is positioned. Though length and type may vary, the one thing all ladders have in common are steps, usually a dozen or so equally distanced rungs that allow the climber to go up and down.

"Climbing the ladder" has been a metaphor in the career world for years. And there was a time that I trusted it enough to climb it too. I trusted that it would make me happy. I trusted that it would make me successful. I trusted that as long as I stayed on it, it would bring me fulfillment. But I found my ladder was leaning on the wrong wall. Whether it be real or metaphorical, if the ladder we're climbing isn't placed properly and anchored securely, regardless if we're on the top rung or not, we still won't reach what we set out to reach.

So it was with me. I thought I was climbing a ladder of success only to learn later that it wasn't taking me at all where I wanted to go. So I jumped off, trusting that my instincts were right and that I could find another way to define and achieve success.

Now that I've been on this new ladder a while, I've found the view is great on many levels, the journey rewarding, and the memories irreplaceable. I hope to encourage you to join me, and to consider the possibility of repositioning your career ladder to another place entirely, rethinking how you define your career and your own personal success, and redefining a clearer, more focused plan for your family.

Steps on the ladder of parenting can be climbed with the same determination and drive that would normally be expected in the pursuit of a career. The work is certainly no less important, influential, or rewarding. Each step can lead us toward recognizing our true value as parents and realizing a vision for our families and ourselves.

The direction in which we lead our families is of paramount importance. Why let our careers overshadow our lives at home, or overtake time with our families, allowing us to stop investing in those we love?

For me, making my family a priority meant stepping away from my career. I couldn't prioritize both my work and my family, and I wonder how many women do it. When I stepped away, I found that the energy I channeled into working toward someone else's goals could now be transferred to working toward my own. And this realization was liberating.

I didn't need to change my level of passion toward my career;
I just had to change how I defined my career.

What if parenting was the most important job I could pursue? How would I approach it? How would it be done successfully? If parenting were a career position, the job description would list the need for dedication, strategic thinking, goal setting, flexibility, creativity, discipline, and long hours. It would be full-time work with no financial pay, no time off, and enormous amounts of stress. On the flip side, the benefits would be terrific (flexible hours, loving clients, world-changing impact).

Perhaps if parenting were, in fact, written out like a job, some of us might have reconsidered before taking it on. Most of us, I would venture to say, had ideas about what parenting meant and were likely surprised when it turned out to be completely different. Certainly once that little person comes into your life and grabs your finger for the first time, or looks you in the eye, all soft and funny-smelling and completely dependent, you're hooked. You become one of those people you swore you'd never be, the kind that talks about their kid as the cutest, smartest, and most promising child you've ever seen.

But parenting is the biggest kind of commitment, and all commitments take time. If we can parent with a clear, defined set of goals and a comprehensive plan, it will help us make the most of that time. And even though, as with any commitment, there is sacrifice required to see bigger goals realized, a parenting life of purpose and discipline can still be fun, challenging, fulfilling, and surprising.

Redefining parenting in the same way as a career does not negate or minimize the important work we may have as nurses, teachers, lawyers, salespeople, executive assistants, or anything else within the workforce. Of course there is important work to be done within the marketplace. The approach I am proposing may not be right for some families. There are many families who struggle to make ends meet and rely on two incomes for even the most basic of needs.

Most of us are not in the situation of wondering where our next meal is coming from and are working for a variety of other reasons. The danger becomes letting our jobs overtake or crowd out our most important roles as parents, spouses, and members within our own communities. None of us wants life to overrun our time with family, yet most of us struggle with the balance of work and family life.

So you see, a ladder built on family success can be every bit as complex as a career one, and there is much to consider before each step is taken. Adjustments need to be made regularly to ensure that the goals you set remain fixed and in sight. With a plan, for ourselves and our families, and goals that are feasible, practical, and meaningful, we can be confident that we will not lose our motivation or our way.

By working our way through a variety of principles, like climbing the steps of a ladder, we can move upward toward the goals we set and ensure that the vision for ourselves and our families comes together harmoniously.

*We don't have to change who we are; we just alter
what we do and how we do it.*

We don't become less ambitious; we simply channel that ambition and drive toward leading and supporting our families instead.

In contrast to the traditional career ladder model that suggests that only those at the top are successful, the ladder I am referring to defines success at each step.

*Getting to the top of this ladder is not the goal, for each step
on the ladder is a journey of growth and goal setting as
unique and individual as you are.*

Being on the ladder and learning from each stage are the objectives, while making sure your ladder is truly anchored by the right things and leaning against the right wall, a wall of your choosing.

I'm convinced we all want successful families, personal satisfaction, and purpose. Leaning our life ladder on something other than just our work encourages us to begin to see the fullness of what we are created to be and do. If we climb the rungs of our life ladder with a fixed goal in mind and are purposeful in achieving the steps required, we can find ourselves in amazing new places we previously thought impossible.

If we take time to consider the importance of our roles as parents, we can see that it is a privilege to lead a family. By being intentional in prioritizing our children and marriages, I believe we can begin to construct much of the personal life and home life we truly want.

"Where did you learn that?"

We don't like the idea of others teaching our kids the important lessons in life. It is natural for parents to want input on how their kids view life's experiences. We want them to see life through the lens we are able to offer, with the wisdom, experience, love, and personal investment that we uniquely bring.

I knew that in order for me to be involved in my son's life to the degree I felt was important, I needed to make an adjustment in how I viewed work. When it came to my son's upbringing, I didn't want to miss a moment of it, and I also never wanted to wonder, as a parent, if I had truly given him the best I had to offer.

To put my son and my family at the top of my priority list meant my career would need to move aside, at least for a while. It would mean taking a leap off my career ladder into an arena where I was initially unprepared and lacking experience. Yet, equipped with skills from years in the marketplace, a desire to make our family thrive, a conviction that the precious years while my son was young were too important to miss, and a leap of faith, I went forward.

Certain short distance runners in Russia leap off ladders as part of their training. This unusual exercise is believed to strengthen the lateral muscles in their legs, making their nerves fire faster so they are less likely to be injured (Christopher McDougall, *Born To Run: A Hidden Tribe, Super Athletes, and the Greatest Race the World Has Never*

Seen [New York: Knopf, 2009]). It makes them terrifically strong and resilient.

Leaping off my career ladder was scary, but as with the runners, it made me stronger in all the areas in my life, not just with my family. It made me more appreciative of what it takes to manage a home and raise children. It allowed me to see life from a different angle and appreciate how much training and effort go into pursuing a life lived well. My family was waiting...all I had to do was leap.

This book is written with two focuses in mind.

1. I believe it is best for children and families for one parent to stay home, and

2. there are important lessons parents should strive to teach their own children.

Finally, I feel it is important to say that I had the opportunity and luxury to make this decision without any significant sacrifices to my lifestyle. I realize that many parents cannot stop working, and that each family has their own dynamics and must make their own decision. Yet, there are questions to consider, and lessons I've learned, that I believe will be helpful regardless of whether you are a working parent or a working-at-home parent. Join me in this discussion and arrive at your own answer to *What If Parenting is the Most Important Job in the World?*

Chapter 1
A New Identity

"Two roads diverged in a wood, and I—I took the one less traveled by, and that has made all the difference."
~ Robert Frost

One of my friends has a little girl named Hanna. "Hanna Banana" is what we call her, except when she decides that she is Princess Ariel, or Princess Jasmine, or one of the other assorted Disney beauties. On those occasions, she will be quick to inform you that she is in fact, for that day, Princess "Whatever." You are not to call her by any other name. She will not respond and will only be annoyed by your insensitivity and ignorance. She is three. Even at three, Hanna is trying to adopt a distinctive identity.

I don't think Hanna is unique. I think we all search for an identity at different points throughout our lives. We identify with where we choose to live, or the sports team we support, or the school we attended, and yes, our career.

That was me. I was like Hanna—trying to find my identity. Only I was seeking it within my career, something unrelated to who I really was.

A New Role

There was a day when the sum value of my identity was defined by the title on my business card. Not anymore. Several years ago, I stepped away from climbing the ladder of a traditional career and began ascending the steps of an entirely different one. I no longer have a traditional career and now work at home, doing whatever this "job" requires.

It's true I have no official job description or title, but I do have as commanding a vision, as clear a focus, and as definitive a purpose as the leader of any Fortune 500 company.

I've discovered that "staying at home" is an honorable job well worth embracing. It's a challenging and rewarding career that requires a great deal of creativity, sensitivity, and breadth. Raising children is far too important to be left to anyone who isn't as committed or invested as we, their parents, are. I didn't want to miss a moment of my son's upbringing, and I didn't feel that his best interests were served by my pursuing a career outside of our home. Even if you can't stay home full time, the lessons I suggest can still be important to consider. I believe the time we all have to invest in our kids is short and the effects long term.

In the midst of raising a family, I believe it can be easy to forget what a privilege it is to be a parent. There are moments, and we've all had them, when parenting feels more like a burden. Raising kids is expensive, time-consuming, tiring, occasionally frustrating, and scary. While we're busy shuttling kids to soccer, helping with homework, changing diapers, or staying up with a sick child, the beauty and blessing of parenting can be lost. Yet, make no mistake about it, getting the opportunity to raise a child is a huge privilege, a gift. Having the chance to witness the growth and life of another person is amazing. We are there to see each level of development, each blessed day, each life-forming experience. It's an astounding journey, a unique and rewarding part of life. Parenthood is a miracle.

Identities

I had always planned on being a mom at some point, yet I feared that being the mom I wanted to be involved more than I was capable of offering. Motherhood looked hard to me. I was not convinced that I would have the skill set needed to do all that I felt was required of being a mother. And I became even more convinced of this after working for ten years and watching other mothers around me. What did I know about parenting? What could I possibly bring to this role? Clearly, if I were to be a mom, and one that "stayed home," it would have to be different than what I had previously envisioned. If I was going to walk away from a career I loved and make parenting my career, I was going to have to define it in my own terms and decide just how I was going to make it the most meaningful and productive time I could spend.

I felt that no one else was as invested as I in my family's future, nor as uniquely qualified, to make our collective goals a reality.

Years into parenthood, I began to assemble a list of life lessons—things I wanted to teach my son that I felt were too important to dismiss. This list now includes principles and guidelines, like the rungs of a ladder that I trust will lead him to be more prepared for his own life journey. They are lessons that I want him to learn as early as possible, practices to claim and own. **Rungs of faith, character, and integrity** that will serve him well when times are tough and the future seems uncertain. **Principles of personal accountability** that will make him strong and unafraid, and someone others can depend on. **Tenets of truth** that will provide wisdom that he can rely on and refer to as he matures and goes his own way.

There is a concept called the principle of prior choice, which refers to the predetermination of what a decision or response will be long before an actual situation presents itself. For example, I can decide ahead of time to be joyful, honest, morally upright, or faithful even when I don't feel like it or the situation is difficult. I can decide my response to many of the big things of life in advance so that I will be prepared when the situations arise and won't be caught off guard. By doing so, I can be confident with a solution, rather than wondering what to do when I'm feeling tired, stressed, alone, or attacked.

The big moral and ethical foundations can be laid in advance, making us strong enough to withstand the tides of circumstance. These foundational blocks set the framework for the way we filter the information we receive and the situations we encounter, emotionally, physically, and spiritually. They give us perspective and help us stay calm and focused when the tendency is not to be.

Likewise, if we are able to set much of the groundwork in our children's lives to include fundamental truths and basic boundaries, they will be more apt to face the future with confidence and character. They can lean on certain principles and feel safe operating within clear boundaries. When they are tempted to cheat or lie, be promiscuous or irresponsible, they will have already made the hard decisions about such things alongside you, with your guidance, perspective, love, and involvement. They will know their response, finding strength and security in that assurance.

When our kids learn the skills for handling life from us, they don't have to look to the culture, classroom, or computer to teach them. They will be secure in who they are and in how important they are to us as their parents.

I'm convinced that most of us don't figure out who we are, what we want, and how we're going to respond to life until much, much later. Meanwhile, we can spend years as adults struggling with basic issues of identity, respect, and meaning. If I can help my son get a jump-start on basic foundational truths, his chances of truly successful living are greatly increased. He won't waste time on things that frustrate or delay and will be living life more fully, intentionally, and purposefully. Life is hard enough without low self-esteem, a lack of moral direction, and a misplaced sense of identity coming into play.

If I can give my son a toolbox of truths and values to frame his life with, he will have much of what he needs as he matures. And so I started with a simple list of twenty life lessons I didn't want to miss teaching my son: principles that would help him build the life he wants for himself and that God has planned for him to lead.

My first lesson was hard....It became the initial reason I wrote this book and why I made a journal of my journey. I spent way too many years of my life focusing on a career I thought defined me, only to find out that it would often disappoint me and ultimately derail me from doing what would really bring me joy. I want to make sure that my son never confuses his choice of a profession with who he is as a person.

Life Lesson #1. Our work is not who we are.

This was a tough one for me. The idea of what I did and who I was got confused for many years. As I made the step away from the professional arena to focus on matters at home, I struggled with the identity part of the transition more than anything else.

I needed to get to a place where my understanding of who I was as a person was not dependent on my job description, professional status, or supposed success in the marketplace.

Getting to that point was, and still is, a process of small and intentional steps toward a specific set of goals. The nature of my role now continues to ebb and flow, but my vision remains clear and my purpose unwavering. I am now on a ladder of my own choosing, directed toward being all that I can be.

For me, this ladder had to be initially established on faith and family. My faith and my love for my family motivate and encourage me when the day seems long and the job thankless. I know that no one can do what I do in the way I do it. I have learned to recognize and appreciate the importance of my own personal contribution, and through it I am motivated to do my best. The contentment I feel and the closeness I see in my family, day by day, week by week, and year by year, give me peace that I've made the right choice for this time in my life.

My family and my faith are stronger because I have made them both priorities.

So, like Hanna, I have chosen to define myself by my own terms. But it is all now about the contribution I make to my family and the difference I can make in the world around me. What I currently do is more than just another *job*—it is a joy-filled, challenging, and rewarding *career*. Taking care of my family is something I cannot imagine anyone else doing. Yet, I had to have a vision I could commit to in order for it to succeed, a vision no one else but me was able to fully see or realize.

A Busy Day

After over a decade of being in the role of "household manager," "stay-at-home mom," or whatever you want to call it, I've found that my day is filled with much more than I ever imagined. Sure, it includes the often mundane tasks of driving, cooking, cleaning, and organizing, but the job also includes facilitating, teaching, leading, supporting, nurturing, cheerleading, and guiding.

This, of course, doesn't take into account the fact that I'm like a doctor on call, likely to be called into service in the middle of the night with a sick child, or late at night helping with a school project, or anything that adds to or changes the schedule. There are no defined hours—it all happens whenever and however my life dictates, that day, that week, or that month.

Despite the odd hours and busy schedule, I have to be purposeful in creating time to do things that energize and rejuvenate my spirit, which for me is being physically active, writing, and making time to be with God. There is so much to do and so few hours in which to do it that most nights I fall asleep completely exhausted because it was a full day.

It's a job that has also changed significantly as my son has grown. The demands on my time have altered from when he was little. I've had to adjust the way I spend my day and the way I parent with each changing year. Obviously, with a fourteen-year-old, I am no longer changing diapers and scheduling around his nap times, but I've found that while the demands are different, they are not necessarily easier.

Not What It Used to Be

Describing my life by just "stay-at-home mom" doesn't begin to describe what I do, or try to do. I certainly don't see myself as a mom from an era of black-and-white televisions, Betty Crocker casseroles, and Jell-O molds. I'm a latte-drinking, recycling, technology-using, millennial mom.

The ideas about and expectations of what a stay-at-home mom should be have changed over the years. I never did know what "staying at home" was initially supposed to imply, but I'm fairly sure that it doesn't look much like what I do now.

The Gap in the Resume (and the Hole in My Ego)

I remember years ago when my husband and I applied for a home mortgage, and, for the first time, I had no definable occupation to list.

"Currently unemployed? Between jobs? Transitional time? Is any of this what they are looking for?" I thought quietly but frantically.

I sat there frozen for a couple of minutes until the awkwardness forced my husband to ask, "Is everything okay?"

"Yeah, yeah," I mumbled. "I just don't know what to put down on this line."

"Oh, *homemaker* will do just fine," quipped the title coordinator.

"That's right, isn't it, because you don't *work.*" The words hung there in space, hovering over the conference table until they entered my brain with a smack.

Not long before, I was armed with a business card, eager to tell everyone and anyone what I did for a living.

Ever since I had made the decision to be home full time with our new son, it felt like I had stumbled into a new career with no respectable job title, no work experience, no pay, and very little respect.

My previous job was *Account Executive*, which was a sales position with a somewhat long and vague title. I actually sold advertising time, or airtime, at various local network television stations in two different markets. My father used to tell his neighbors that I was an *Executive Accountant*, which only proved that he must have misunderstood my job from the very beginning. He had no idea what I really did (sell air?), causing his neighbors to mistakenly ask me for tax advice each and every April. That should have been a clue to me early on that it was silly to identify myself with my job or job title.

Television sales was a good career choice for a young woman in her twenties, and I loved it. It was an unusual job with a lot of growth and financial potential. I had an expense account, a car phone (back when it was a big deal), regular lunch appointments, a busy social calendar, and professional club memberships. For many years I proudly displayed the television station logo on a license tag on the front of my car. I was completely dedicated. I loved feeling needed and part of a team. My sales results were responsible for much of the operation of the station. I had clients around town that I called friends. I had even considered that, at one point, I would remain single and throw myself completely into my career, pursuing it as far as it would take me. By my late twenties, I was interviewing in large broadcast markets around the country. I felt like I was on my way.

But, life frequently has a way of changing your plans. When my husband, Ken, walked into my life, my whole world and viewpoint began to change. I began reevaluating everything in my life when I met that tall, lanky young man, with the biggest blue eyes I'd ever seen, in a new church I was attending. Ours was a whirlwind romance. In three short months we were engaged, and three months later we were married. Suddenly, in the span of six months, I was viewing everything within the framework of two instead of one. It was exciting and romantic but a broad and all-encompassing change for both of us.

His career was flying higher and faster than mine and so became the primary factor in the choices we made in regard to where we lived, what our plans as a couple and family would be, and how we would attack the challenges ahead of us. It also started to alter my idea of what my career meant and how I viewed success.

Moving and Learning

Months after we were married, Ken's company relocated their headquarters and we were expected to move to Dallas. There wasn't much time to think about it. We would move within thirty days because Ken's job was taking us there. Although somewhat exciting and adventurous, moving was still scary and meant leaving my hometown and living six hours away.

Our plans as a couple would now be within the context of living away from family. This was the first time I'd done that. Ken had friends within the company that were part of the move, but my friends and both sides of the family would not be there. Mostly, it would be just the two of us figuring out a new town and a new life together.

So, we adopted a team mentality. I would handle the details of our move while he settled into his new environment at work. I would manage the process of building a new house while he assisted and supported me in all the related decisions. I would table my career for the time being and focus on the matters at hand while he went ahead with his career. I assumed there would be time to interview for jobs later, and I would have ample time to scope out the media landscape and plan my attack beforehand.

Ken and I shared similar desires for raising a family. Both of us had been brought up in fairly traditional families, with our moms staying home during our childhoods. Yet we acknowledged that the world was different now. We weren't sure how that traditional model applied to us, but it seemed there would be plenty of time to work out the details when the time came.

A Different Era

Parents in the 1950s, 1960s, and early 1970s were living in different times. In 1970, 85% of children lived at home with both their mother and father. Now, forty years later, only 67% do. In 1970, the majority of women in America worked in some capacity outside the home, although most were not employed full time.

In 2010, over 65 million working moms are employed full time, with a record 59% having infants under the age of one.

When World War II ended in 1945, many women quit factory and military jobs, and with servicemen back home, wives turned their focus to family matters. With that, the famous "baby boom" was born. In the decades that followed, women began a steady return to the workplace, newly armed with trade skills and college educations, and forever changed the landscape of the American family. Women were working, often completely through their child-rearing years.

In 1970, 50% of children came home directly from school to someone waiting for them. Now only 30% do.

As girls growing up in those postwar decades, we were beginning to form our opinions of what a motherly role looked like. For those of us who had moms at home, it was nice having room mothers, block mothers, and moms at PTA and fun night. But as young college graduates, many of us were skeptical about the "staying home" role; we were unsure that it was "our thing." We felt we could and should do something more meaningful and significant than "just" being a mom. After all, we had an education; we had opportunity. We liberated women had the whole package.

Thankfully not everyone bought into that idea. There were many young, bright, driven female college students that planned all along on making family a priority. My college roommate, Susan, was one of them. But that wasn't me, and it wasn't many of the women I knew.

After the sexual revolution of the 1960s, women flooded into the workplace in droves, motivated by their sense of newly found independence and the economy of the 1970s. Today, working women represent 50% of the United States workforce, and 70% of married moms are working in some capacity outside the home, reflecting a trend that had been increasing every year since America became a nation (U.S. Census, 2006). However, in the year 2002, something strange happened. The percentage of working women peaked and started a decline.

Could this reflect that parents are discovering a new identity outside the traditional workforce? Have our priorities changed, with parents wanting to more fully experience all that family can be? Is keeping family as a focus a balancing act that is too difficult to manage?

I think it might be all of those things.

As a young college graduate in the 1980s, my plan involved earning my own money so that I could get my own place, buy a nice car, and not have to depend on anyone financially. Being completely independent was something my father placed a high value on. I assumed that at some point in the future, I would neatly fit the perfect husband, two kids, house, and dog into the perfect life.

At twenty-two, I officially entered the workplace, only discovering several years later that my big plans weren't playing out the way I had hoped. The goals I initially set were more guided by what I *thought* success looked like than what success really involved. Simply having a career wasn't going to bring me the fulfillment I sought. Naturally I wanted the career, but I also wanted a family with someone I could love helping me to grow into the woman I wanted to be. I didn't want to embrace some unrealistic idea of being a super-woman that could have it all and do it all, but that is exactly what I did. Yet, there was a part of me that questioned the assumption that women could only find happiness by achieving more, earning more, and doing more.

I may have thought it sounded fishy, but back then, I still bought into it, hook, line, and sinker.

Years later, after I was married to Ken and committed to the idea of full-time parenting, I realized that such a concept meant venturing into new territory where I would need a lot of help. I had now come to a new place in life with new goals and a new focus. Yet, it felt like I was jumping off one ladder and contemplating climbing another. Was I really going to stop working and focus on things at home with the same intensity? Was that really the way to start?

I really didn't have a clue how to begin. I needed a vision and I needed it now.

Eventually my husband and I talked more specifically about how we saw ourselves as a couple and a family, and how my working (or not working) matched up with that. Our initial conversation was a starting point, but just a baby step in laying out what would become a very broad set of goals.

We knew that if we were going to have a clear and meaningful vision for what my specific role included, we had to know what it would look like practically and physically. We would need a way to quantify whether or not we as a family were heading in the right direction.

I am a woman who likes a plan. I am not spontaneous. I'm not saying this is entirely a good thing; in fact it can be quite annoying to those closest to me. My husband likes surprises. I do not. Ken likes to take the road less traveled. I like to stay on the highway. I am into the details, and I really, really like to know what to expect.

So, for me, I knew that in order for me to step away from the work world and do something as unstructured as "staying at home," I was going to have to have a clear and workable plan. And even with such a plan, there was no guarantee of success or promise that it was going to be easy.

Before I became pregnant, having a conversation, creating a vision, and considering that kind of decision seemed easy.

*Once the actual day came, and I walked away from my career
by turning down a lucrative dream job, the whole decision
became another matter entirely.*

You see, I was offered a job at one of the top television stations in the country, a job I had always wanted that I thought fit me to a tee. Ironically, the week I got the call offering me the position was the same week I found out I was pregnant. I found myself at a crossroad. I couldn't start such a job knowing I might quit after nine months, and I couldn't see throwing myself into a new job while also being a new mother. I knew I had to turn the job down if I was really going to make my family the priority I said I wanted it to be.

But that, as you might imagine, wasn't so easy to do. I remember that day well: making that tough call, placing the phone back in the cradle, sitting down on the floor of my bedroom, and having a good cry. There was a part of me that was so disappointed, so confounded that I had to make such a choice. I didn't even know what motherhood required, but I knew that I had made that prior choice—to be home with a baby should I be blessed enough to have one—and I was sticking to it, even if it was hard.

Having the decision made in advance didn't mean I wasn't riddled with doubts and questions.

What was I thinking?

What am I doing?

Is this crazy?

I'm scared to death.

Shouldn't I think about this some more?

Nearly all of my friends were working moms. I really didn't have girlfriends that stayed home with their kids. I didn't know anyone my age to ask for advice. And now that I was pregnant and the decision needed to be made, I needed help.

As a big reader, I went looking for resources in the local library and bookstore to help me navigate this new terrain. There were a few books and articles, but I felt that most were outdated and generally didn't address the specific challenge of leaving the work world.

When my literary search turned up unsuccessful, I considered my own upbringing, specifically my mother, the only model I personally had any working knowledge of. Though she certainly was a good model, surely there was a way to take her example from decades ago and update it. I just couldn't see myself parenting the same way my parents had.

I was also convinced that I had learned valuable skills from all those years in the workplace and that those same abilities could and would translate to what I was attempting to do here. That's where I should begin, I concluded.

I would take the basic workplace model and apply it to the home and family situation: transcribe the professional formula to fit a personal one.

And so the creative process began. I mulled things over at two o'clock in the morning while I was sitting in a rocker feeding my son. I jotted down notes while I was at a playground watching other mothers and their kids. I contemplated while I was on the treadmill, trying to get my pre-baby body back. I did a lot of observing, considering, planning, and thinking.

After a while, I concluded that though the traditional "stay at home" model is a good one in basic structure, I needed it to be updated and clarified. In order for me to fully wrap my arms around the idea, it would need to be defined with goals for my family, specifically designed to meet the changing needs of each of us.

And it went beyond just my family and my experience. I started to expand the basic idea and envision a more global family model that prioritized time parents spent with their children while being sensitive to the demands on families today.

I was convinced that my fearfulness, my hesitation, and my anxiety were not unique to my experience. There was a lot to learn about making this transition, and I was not alone in it. And as I traversed across the landscape of this life-stage, I would be able to give a viewpoint to others at various stages of the journey and perhaps encourage them to travel it with me.

So, what did my plan look like, and what kind of mission was I suggesting?

Chapter 2
A New Choice

"Vision without action is merely a dream. Action without vision just passes the time. Vision with action can change the world."
~ Joel Barker

"We are losing our kids," writes a teacher and mother. "Each year they are coming to us more ill prepared to meet the needs of school socially and academically."

A friend of mine, after many years of teaching, shared with me that the single greatest influence on each of her students was the strain she sensed within their families. Based on her experience teaching in a public school in a middle-class suburb of Detroit, her conclusion was that many families today are hurting and struggling—financially, emotionally, spiritually, and morally. As a result, many kids today are distracted, tired, over-medicated, over-scheduled, and more isolated than ever.

Today there are 74 million kids in the United States under the age of eighteen and 20 million kids under the age of five.

That's a lot of kids to consider (U.S. Census, 2006).

Today's children spend more time in front of a screen than they ever do personally interacting with their families or friends. Some research suggests that teens today spend as much as forty to fifty hours a week on the computer or watching television (http://news. yahoo.com). Other studies show that toddlers, particularly those in home-based daycare, are watching as much as two hours a day, in addition to the two to three hours a day they already watch at home (Dimitri Christakis, "Early Television Exposure & Subsequent Attentional Problems in Children," *Pediatrics Journal* 113, no. 4 [2004]: 708–13). That's one-third of the time they are awake each day.

All this time in front of the computer and using the cell phone has led to some startling statistics. According to a recent study, nearly 40% of teens today have sent sexually related messages to others (sexting), and an alarming 20% of all teens have taken nude pictures of themselves and sent them to others via their cell phone or computer (www.cosmogirl.com). While there are young people who are given parameters for time spent alone or in front of a screen, there are scores of young adults and children who are not. Around 25% of school-age children in America are "latch key." No one is home when they get out of school, and the television and internet are there to use without supervision. As many as 40% of middle-school-aged teens in two-income families are unsupervised after school (www.latchkey-kids.com).

Lonely young people turn to the internet for friendship and socialization. Others turn to food for entertainment and acceptance. In light of our nation's 33% obesity rate among children and teens, this is also a troubling concern ("The Depressed Child," *American Academy of Child and Adolescent Psychiatry*, no. 4 [2008], www.aacp.org).

Most are also spiritually adrift, susceptible to whatever current of contemporary thought surrounds them. We live in a world full of religious ideas and cultures and most of them are given full rights and expression within our own public schools. While many may embrace this fullness of diversity, statistics show that the pluralism can be confusing to our kids. Young people easily absorb a multi-ethnic and multi-belief worldview. But all religious systems are not created equal, and our kids are looking to us to help them navigate the variety of religious information and traditions they encounter.

And while many children are learning to succeed in the classroom and on the sports field, not enough are learning to succeed in life. Unmonitored and unsupervised, they grow up unprepared for the challenges ahead of them and are likely to cry out to their parents in a variety of ways.

Frightening Statistics

Statistics reflect what I think our hearts already know. Too much of the enormously important job of raising our kids is getting shifted to others who aren't as personally or emotionally invested, or aren't as capable of giving kids what they really need. A generation is in danger of being lost while parents watch from a distance.

Children today are more given to depression, loneliness, suicide, teen pregnancy, and violence than ever before. One in eight teens is depressed, with only 30% getting any kind of help for it. Statistics on teen sexual activity are very troubling. The United States leads the Western industrialized world in the number of teen pregnancies, with 34% of young women getting pregnant before the age of twenty, and 80% which are unintended pregnancies of unwed mothers (www.familyfirstaid.org).

An overly busy life and rampant materialism can make kids feel that they are an unimportant part of the family and disposable to society. They lack sufficient moral direction and don't look to us, as their parents, to guide and direct them when they do get into trouble. Without adequate parental counsel, they lean on friends and peers to help them make big life decisions, which can often lead to even bigger issues and more bad decisions.

I believe that if kids have holes in their lives where their parents should be, they will not know what is missing and will try to fill it somehow. They will pursue anything or anyone that offers acceptance and meaning, and when they don't find it, they will despair and act out in all kinds of ways against themselves, each other, and society.

We read the headlines all too often—kids bringing guns or home-made bombs to school, attacking others, or taking their own lives, and almost always, we find out afterward that there were warning signs or cries for help beforehand. All across our country, kids are acting out in aggression toward their schools, their parents, and themselves, and we are shocked and saddened by it. But we think and hope we are immune when often we're not. We cross our fingers and wish for the best, and we hope that our family doesn't become a statistic and our kids will turn out okay. While we certainly can't control everything that our kids do or become, we can be deliberate in our commitment to them and be purposeful about setting high ethical and moral standards. We can create models they can pattern, and we can offer a grid of wisdom that they can filter life through. We can give them parameters to live within that offer them the safety and security they desire.

It's true we can't give them everything, but we can give them our love and our time, since that's all they really want anyway.

Of course, I would be misleading if I suggested that violent actions of teens are directly related to parents working outside the home. A variety of research shows that inappropriate behavior, in whatever way it manifests itself, has more to do with the parents' involvement in their lives than the overall household income level. Kids from well-to-do households are just as likely to be troubled as those from lower-income homes. Putting kids in a better school district, bigger house, or nicer neighborhood does not ensure that they won't be confronted with challenges in their peer groups.

"The scholarly evidence, in short, suggests that at the heart of the explosion of crime in America is the loss of the capacity of fathers and mothers to be responsible for caring for the children they bring into the world," writes Patrick Fagan, PhD (www.heritage.org).

I want to do all I can as a parent to make sure my son doesn't feel he has to prove anything to his peers, to society, or to me or his father. I want to equip him with the tools he will need to deal with peer pressure, shifting moral standards in our culture, and his naturally budding sense of independence. I want to give him boundaries that don't stifle him but guide him in learning to make his own wise choices. I also want to be consistent in my messages to him—living out what I preach and teach. And I want him to know, as every parent does, that my love for him is not dependent on his performance in the sports arena, in the classroom, or anywhere.

One of the things crucial to our children's success in this world is their ability to handle adversity. Adversity will come to every one of us, regardless of position, education, or experience. The earlier we can learn how to handle the trials of life, the better.

Life Lesson #2. How to handle adversity.

How we handle the trials in our life speaks to our character. There are many who let the "falling downs" of this world derail them from an otherwise fulfilling and productive existence. They allow the setbacks and failures to become a disability, subsequently robbing them of happiness and meaning.

My son will lose and he will win. He will cry and laugh, stumble and run. Life is full of balance. If he is unprepared to handle half of what he will face in life, he will be at a disadvantage for sure, and he will spend much of his life frustrated, fatigued, and feeling like a failure. Learning how to handle adversity is huge.

Our responsibility as parents requires time, talent, and patience. Learning how to read, diagram sentences, or multiply fractions is just part of the learning our kids do at school. Much of their education is done in the hallways, in locker rooms, on buses, and at playgrounds. It's a battlefield out there, and kids, just like adults, are sadly not always good, nice, or fair. Many a lesson has been learned and shared after the school day is over.

I'm glad that I am there to troubleshoot those confrontations before and after school, to help my son navigate those situations and put the events of the day into perspective. If I am hurried, distracted, or preoccupied, I will miss the opportunity to help and teach.

A parent has traveled the road of childhood and adolescence and has been in unpleasant and awkward circumstances. We've lived through the temptations, trials, and tests. As adults, we know how it all plays out in the end; a young person often doesn't. We can offer perspective and comfort, guidance and humor. But we can only do that if we are present.

Life Lesson #3. A parent's love is unconditional.

I have witnessed many a sports parent at the soccer field, natatorium, or arena forget that their child is not there to fulfill their own personal ambitions of greatness. My son is a swimmer. Performance is measured by tenths of seconds. The blink of an eye can be the difference between winning and losing. The slightest miscalculation of the kick of a ball or the strike of a puck can become a defining moment for a young person who feels that he has let down his parents, his coach, and his teammates. Yet the very same situation can also be a learning opportunity in handling defeat and disappointment with dignity and grace. How we handle each life lesson is up to us, and what we teach our kids in the process is undeniable.

Now, for the record, I'm not a proponent of awarding a trophy to everyone, regardless of their ability or performance, but I do acknowledge that some parents need a huge dose of perspective when it comes to their kids' participation in sports. This subject could warrant an entire book of its own, but suffice it to say, I personally know that whatever success my son has in swimming or anything else has to come from his own heart, his own will, and his own determination.

When asked if she had ever imagined her son, Michael, would be considered the greatest Olympic swimmer of all time, Debbie Phelps stated that it was never her dream; it was always Michael's. She saw many parents pushing their kids for the wrong reasons in a sport they hated because it was the ambition of the parent, not the child.

The most important thing I want my son to remember about swimming, regardless of how "successful" he is, is that he learned the valuable lessons of hard work, discipline, teamwork, and humility, and that regardless of what the scoreboard or stopwatch said, he was still my son, greatly loved and highly valued. The medals were fine, but the manner in which he participated was more important to me and would be ultimately to him.

Parenting doesn't happen in a vacuum. I have to spend time with my son in order for all of what I want him to learn to actually be flushed out and exhibited. I can't just tell him what I want him to learn; I have to show it, live it out, and have it tested and tried through my own trials and difficulties. And of course, all of that takes time.

My own experience has led me to believe that what we need to give our kids is simply "time." Time to let conversations come freely and time to have our kids see us react to the world around us in a variety of situations. They need time to watch and learn who we are, and to have fun, relax, dream, and play with us. They don't require highly scheduled time, just time. We need time to let things happen organically, not feeling like a few minutes in the car on the way to daycare or school are, in and of themselves, really going to create the kind of closeness with our kids we need and desire. Time in the car can be time well spent, but it shouldn't be the *only* time spent. And time with our kids should be purely that…time with our kids. Undistracted, unrushed, dedicated time spent investing in them.

I believe my friend is right; we are losing our kids.

And along with that, we're losing ourselves. We're busy, distracted, and unhappy. A recent study out of the University of Pennsylvania's Wharton School says that women are more unhappy than ever and that our happiness has been eroding steadily since the 1970s (www.elle.com).

Research shows that moms today are spending only two hours a day with their children (AOL/OMD Global Moms study: "Living La Vida Rapida: Parents Living a Double Life at Double Time," 2008). This same research found mothers spending just under five hours a day on television and the internet, and less than half as much time cooking meals and cleaning the house as they did forty years ago. While the mothers of 1960 may not have been perfect themselves, today's mothers clearly are not making enough time for "quality time." Thanks to the wonders of the information age, we are able to do more than ever before, but the challenge is finding that balance between tasks completed and life lived. They are not the same thing. Television and the internet can be huge distractions. I do a lot of research, writing, and corresponding on the internet, but I also know that I have, all too frequently, been tempted to waste time on the computer. I have to catch myself and be reminded that it is time I won't get back, and it's not time spent with or directly benefiting my family.

> *"In this life we cannot do great things.*
> *We can only do small things with great love."*
> *~ Mother Teresa*

The To-Do List

I'm your usual Type A personality. I expect to do a lot each day, and I am prone to measure myself by the amount of things I am able to check off my list. Sadly, for me it can often determine a good day or a bad day. When my husband asks, "How was your day?" my response is determined by "the list." Lots of check marks equals a good day. Few check marks, a not-so-good day.

My son has no interest in the to-do list I make every day, although I have, on multiple occasions, attempted to impress him with the sheer volume of things I was able to accomplish while he was at school. As far as he's concerned, my day begins when I first see him in the morning and goes on some sort of cosmic hiatus when I drop him off at school. To him, at 3:15, my life magically resumes. He is usually willing and eager to share what *his* day looked like, but he has minimal interest in how mine was spent during those hours.

Generally, as far as my son is concerned, the only time that matters is the time I spend with him. Time is the only commodity that has any value in his eyes.

Our time management and our priorities can easily slip out of balance. No one starts out with the intention of making other things more important than their families; it just happens...one decision at a time.

A Real Example

Diane was a working mom, a busy career woman at a large automotive company. She spent long hours at her job, understandably nervous because of the struggling industry conditions. After months of long hours at the office, she started to put on a few pounds and developed back problems. She realized that she had to do something, so she joined a health club and began going to fitness classes a few nights a week. Her husband worked long hours too, so most nights it meant picking up the kids at daycare, feeding them dinner at the snack bar of the health club or in the car with fast food, and then checking them into childcare for another couple of hours as she rushed to make her aerobics class or personal training session. Afterward, exhausted from a full day at work and a workout, she picked up her two exhausted kids—who hadn't seen either parent all day except for short periods in the car while being ferried between various caretakers, and who were understandably cranky and over-stimulated—and she drove them home, only to tuck them into bed so that they could start the next day all over again.

Diane wants to be a good mother. She didn't prioritize other things above spending time with her children because she hates spending time with them—she was simply responding to life and the difficult challenges in front of her, but she was making choices without stopping to ask herself if they really made sense.

Many parents go through the motions of pursuing personal career goals, independence, hobbies, and even education, and leave everyone behind who doesn't fit into that personal plan. Spouses, kids, family— there is no time for them; there is barely time for themselves. Life becomes the proverbial treadmill, with one day rolling into another, and before we know it, we've drifted far away from where we actually wanted to be.

Pursuing career options and wanting more for ourselves and our kids is not wrong. I believe the methods by which we often pursue them are...and that's what I'm really talking about. If we communicate to our kids that they are not part of an important overall vision for the family and that their training and nurturing can be provided primarily by a nanny or daycare, when other options are available, they learn to adopt that as part of their identity. They look at themselves and their value within the family in a less significant way, which could translate into how they raise families of their own. The cycle can and often does perpetuate itself. On and on it goes, threatening to develop generations of young people unsure of their own intrinsic worth and unprepared for the challenges that life will throw at them.

And yet the parents who dared to stay at home while the rest of the world went on to do "big things" were slapped with an overly simplistic label and made to feel like they weren't working.

I feel the irony is that the parents decades ago who were home for their kids were probably closer to getting the balance right. These days, we are living with sobering statistics about our kids and the state of the family. Prioritizing our family lives will be an important part of changing the culture. I can't say that I'm unhappy with the state of things I see around me if I'm not willing to step up and make the hard choices within my own life. For me, the hard choices included sacrificing the status of a career I loved, relinquishing the financial benefit it would afford, and redefining how I was going to view my value to others.

Guilt Complex

Sadly, I've not met a working mother who hasn't at some time battled a guilt complex about her choice to work. Regardless of how successful or noble the profession or how lucrative the paycheck, there always crops up a nagging feeling in the back of her mind that she somehow is a bad person, is being selfish, or is hopelessly trapped. And no mother I have ever met wants to be a bad mom. No one. It's simply not in our DNA. I think God wires mothers to want to succeed and be fulfilled in this all-important role.

Working moms are under more pressure now than ever.

One in every seven working women is now taking on a second job just to make ends meet (Mother's Day survey, www.careerbuilder.com). This is not an easy decision for anyone. Times are not what they were, and the reality of life sometimes dictates that a mom must work for the basic needs to be met.

The good news here is that working now is defined in entirely different ways. And even moms already at home are finding additional ways to contribute to the financial health of their families by working from home.

It may be a reality that you need to work, but perhaps there are alternative sources of income to consider, varied ways of defining work, and creative ways to provide income that you haven't previously considered.

Guilt can be a destructive emotion, but it can also get our attention. It works like an internal compass telling us that something isn't right or a change needs to be made.

It might be telling us that something is out of alignment and needs to be reconsidered. The key is finding the balance between living the life you were meant to live and doing it in such a way that brings harmony.

"Commit to the Lord whatever you do, and your plans will succeed."
~ Proverbs 16:3

"Honey, the TV Isn't Working Again"

I'm the technical one in our family. In my husband's mind, years of working in the television industry somehow qualifies me to be able to fix and understand all things electronic. I'm not bad at it either. I can usually, often with the help of a manual, troubleshoot most problems we encounter with our computer, stereo system, and various entertainment items.

I like to take the credit for fixing things too, even if it was a really minor problem. I like making it sound like it was a bigger deal than it was. Honestly, half of the problems I run into are solved with one simple task: restarting. Rebooting works wonders. And I often think that we need to reboot and restart in areas of our life as well.

I think there are a lot of us having trouble living out the life we want and seeing the family we desire, and we've found ourselves with overly complicated lives and fashionable but forgotten kids. Getting a fresh start is what we really need.

I am not claiming to be the perfect spouse or parent. Just ask my family. For me, this transition has been hard, and it still continues to be a challenge from time to time, even though I'm deeply convinced it's the right thing to do. But I do get passionate when I see what I consider to be so many people working so hard and simply wearing themselves out; investing in small things that don't matter while letting the big things of life slip away. We, as a network of moms and dads, are sharing the challenge of parenting together, and I appreciate the efforts being made to raise kids in what is a difficult culture and time. Yet there is always room for improvement in every family, and if we carefully evaluate our own situation and are honest about our motives, I am convinced we can turn the cultural tide one family at a time. We can make our families counter-cultural without necessarily cloistering ourselves from culture itself. We can't control the influences around us, but we can control how we respond to them.

Every day we make choices that affect where we go tomorrow—physically, mentally, spiritually, and emotionally. These choices lead us closer to or farther from where we ultimately want to be. They either take us toward a worthy goal or take us off track. They either start propelling us toward a life of meaning or lead us to a life wasted.

We don't need life coaches to teach us this is true—we know it...but we might need reminding.

This book is about setting that vision for ourselves and our families and providing ways to start taking baby steps, if necessary, toward getting there. There are real and practical ways to start making small but significant changes in the way we lead our families and live our lives. It's worth our time and our careful consideration because we're losing our kids...and we're losing ourselves.

"You can shower a child with presents or money, but what do they really mean, compared to the most valuable gift of all—your time? Vacations and special events are nice, but so often the best moments are the spontaneous ones. Being there. Every moment you spend with your child could be the one that really matters."
~ Tim Russert, former American TV journalist

Now What?

Obviously simply "staying home" is not the singular goal—it's what we do with ourselves and on behalf of our families with our time that matters.

One tangible and practical way to begin your journey is to put your initial goals in writing.

Having goals written down greatly increases the likelihood that they will be accomplished. So, start by putting down what you envision for your family and for yourself. Like a company's mission statement, it becomes the grid through which the decisions of your life filter. Post it on your fridge, tuck it in your wallet, or tape it on your bathroom mirror. This vision reminds you of your goals and why you're making certain choices. All successful companies and organizations write mission statements to set the vision, unify the purposes, and help make the decision-making process more efficient. It keeps the employees on the same page. Without them, the direction is unclear, the goal unfixed and fuzzy. I started to expand this basic idea and envision a broader family model that prioritized time parents spend with their children while being sensitive to the demands on the diverse spectrum of families today.

Each family's mission statement is individually tailored to fit your unique set of circumstances. No family is just like yours. Therefore, yours should be personalized, clear, and concise, and it should contain all that you want your family and you to be. The mission statement involves everyone in your home, so leave out no one. Make sure it's a plan everyone can wrap his or her arms around, that it's not just your own idea of an ideal family. You will soon find there is something powerful about committing such ideas to paper. It's the starting block of what can be a remarkable family transformation.

For example, begin by asking yourself the following questions:

1. How do I want my kids to remember me and our time together?

2. What do I want my family to stand for (truthfulness in every situation, loyalty, forgiveness)?

3. How do I want my family to be different from others (friendlier, more close-knit, more generous with our time and talents)?

4. What unique qualities do I bring to this family (musical ability, athletic talent, the gift of communication)?

5. What role do I see my husband/children's father playing in their lives (provider, protector, leader, one who pushes us to do new things)?

6. What would I like us to be known for (our generosity, our graciousness, our involvement, our kindness, our humor, our faithfulness)?

7. What key words would describe my idea of the perfect family (loving, devoted, flexible, humble)?

8. What roles do others within our family dynamic play (grandparents, other extended family, friends)?

9. Where is our family spiritually (head but not heart knowledge, lacking devotion and discipline, growing together toward knowing God)?

10. What would I put as a top priority for our family today? What priority do I see in the next year, two years, five years (finding a church home, getting more involved in our community, spending more time together recreating and playing)?

Then set up questions that apply to your family members:

1. What do you appreciate about our family? What makes it unique?

2. What role do you play within the family?

3. What do you think are our family's strengths? Weaknesses?

4. Would you move to a smaller house if it created a stronger family?

5. If you could change one thing about the way we live, what would it be?

6. Do you know a family that you admire? What is it about them that appeals to you?

7. How would you describe our family spiritually?

8. What significant thing might you do to contribute more to the family?

9. How do you feel about living with fewer material possessions? What can we do without?

10. What is one thing you wouldn't want to change?

These are just seeds to plant in the soil of your mind. Let them germinate and grow into your unique flowering family ideal. Try to think of how this ideal affects everyone in your family. What would they prioritize? What would they want? If you're a spiritual person, ask yourself what God would want to see within your family.

You can make it a family evening exercise. Have the younger members of your family go through magazines and cut out pictures of families that appeal to them, and ask them why they do. Brainstorm different words that you feel describe your family now and words that you would like to see apply to your family in the future. Make it fun and know that there is no wrong way to go about it.

This is how you can begin crafting a family mission statement. As you pare your items down and define your priorities you may find that what your family desires is different than what you initially expected. As you revisit the statement from time to time, you may find it needs to be revised or fine-tuned as ideas become clearer. But if everyone contributes, they are all committed to seeing it happen. If it truly is the vision you see for your family, then it should become essential to each decision you each make.

In addition, consider crafting a mission statement of your own, as it applies to you specifically. For example, this is mine:

> My goal is to raise my child in an unconditionally loving environment that nurtures and encourages him to be what God intends. I will love and support my husband, respecting his role in our marriage, and together, we will create a home of truth and integrity that is a safe haven for everyone and that exhibits our love for the Lord. In all things, I will remember what a high value God places on me, and I will care for and nurture my own self. I will remember that I am not alone in my journey as a stay-at-home mom, that God sees all that I do and try to do. He will give me the needed strength, wisdom, and encouragement if I just seek Him. I also believe that when we as a

family truly seek God's will for our lives, we will be blessed by knowing His peace.

I find that if I read or consider this each day and if I pray for God's help in seeing it through, I am able to keep the right focus, the right state of mind, and the right attitude, since that's where it all begins. I am able to enjoy and remember the purpose of my journey.

"There is a subtle difference between a mission and a promise. A mission is something you strive to accomplish—a promise is something you are compelled to keep. One is individual, the other shared. When a mission and a promise are one and the same... that's when mountains are moved and races are won."
~ Hala Moddelmog, Arby's president

Experiencing the Journey

The beauty of the parenting career involves far more than just goal planning and strategic living; it is laced with beautiful and memorable moments that often seem insignificant but become threads in the fabric of life. When I asked my son, who is now fourteen, what he recalled most from his early childhood, he gave me different memories than I would have listed. He doesn't recall all the hours I did flashcards with him, that I read to him when he was a baby, or that I struggled to maintain a regular schedule that he could depend on. What he remembers are the trips to the park and picnics that were unplanned, occasional day trips to the science center or zoo, and the "sick and rainy" box (a cardboard box filled with little games and activities I would pick up at the consignment store or garage sales and hide until a sick or rainy day came).

He remembers that we made chocolate chip cookies when it snowed and that I was there watching him, encouraging him, taking him to his first swim lessons, soccer practices, and piano lessons, and trying to share my love for tennis by tossing balls over the net to him on summer evenings. He remembers me going to night school to get my master's degree, and then remembers beaming with pride as he watched me walk across the stage to get my cape. He remembers that going to the car wash was a fun event since he could watch the cars go through as he stood by the window, and it was usually accompanied by a trip to Wendy's for lunch.

Does he remember that I helped teach him the fifty states so that he could identify them on a map? No, he just remembers that he could. Does he remember that I took him to story time at the library each and every week without fail? No, he just remembers that he could read at a very early age. Does he remember that I took him in the baby jogger nearly every day for my run? No, he just remembers that I did a lot of running and that he now loves to run, too. He doesn't remember the often difficult and mundane daily routine; he just treasures the results. He still loves to read, he still swims and runs, and he still expects something special to happen on rainy days.

Yesterday was a snow day here in Ohio. School was canceled due to weather. It was one of those delightful surprise days that kids love that can throw parents' plans into a tizzy. Though I know this can be so difficult for working families to shift the daily routine, you might find it is a blessing in disguise to stay home or work from home while spending precious time with your children in a fun activity that you might never have had a chance to experience.

One undeniably big benefit about our lives being structured this way is the freedom and flexibility it affords. My son played outside with a neighbor boy and was able to spend time talking to me about school and the current events in the paper he read, and together we watched a show on the Discovery Channel that we'd never seen before—all because I had the ability to shift gears at a moment's notice and be completely with him at home today.

Even now, as my life is shifting into spending less of my day focusing on the moment-by-moment care of a little one and more time negotiating the schedule of a teenager, I am able to make time for my own personal goals while not compromising the time I spend with him. For instance, I take my notebook computer to the pool while he has swim practice. He swims, I write. I find that if I write when he is home, I miss things. I don't talk with him. He feels he is bothering me. We get disconnected. But here, I can look up occasionally and see him swimming by, back and forth for lap after lap. He knows I'm here but that I'm doing my own thing.

I can't put a dollar amount on the time I have with him. He's fourteen now. In four short years he'll leave for college. In one year he'll start driving. Sometimes it's hard to get my head around it. Forty-eight months and he's not under our roof anymore. I can't believe it. How these last fourteen years have flown. And if you ask any parent, chances are they'll tell you the same. It sounds cliché, but you just don't realize it until it happens to you. You go from not being able to sleep through the night because you're up every two hours when they are infants to the ultra-busy years of talking and toddling and learning the world around them. Then they are off to school, and something happens to the clock at that point—it seems to go twice as fast. In very short order, they're in middle school and before you know it, high school and the college frenzy are upon you.

At the University of Michigan, they used to have a clock at the natatorium counting down the time in hours, minutes, and seconds until the 2008 Olympics (where Michael Phelps would eventually have his remarkable eight gold medal performances). We visited the pool often for clinics and camps, and as the years went by, it struck me that that clock looked like you had all the time in the world—until the last year. Then it seemed time was shrinking at an alarming rate.

And I think that's how it is for us as parents. We think when our kids are really little that we have all the time in the world to get things together, to save for college, to spend time with them...until we realize that by our capricious use of time, we have in fact far less than we thought we did. Suddenly we're in a situation where we only have a few years left with them, and we wish we could do it all over again.

And so, I speak to the urgency of where we are as parents. Not to alarm or depress anyone but to remind us all that *each day matters,* and each decision we can make to give us more time with our kids is a good one.

We each have a purpose in life, and it doesn't necessarily wait until it's comfortable or convenient.

Chapter 3
A New Mission

"Make your life a mission, not an intermission."
~ Arnold Glasgow

Steven Curtis Chapman, singer and songwriter, father and husband, understands the viewpoint of a mother who is feeling overwhelmed and out of control. The lyrics of his song "One Heartbeat at a Time" speak to the unmistakable importance of the time we spend with our children and how easy it is, in the busyness of the day, to get discouraged.

He writes, "So you fall into bed when you run out of hours and you wonder if anything worth doing got done. And maybe you just don't know or maybe you've forgotten. You are changing the world, one little heartbeat at a time."

Stay-at-home parents, I believe, are a somewhat silent, unseen, unheralded force within every community. Every day millions of parents—over five million at the last census—choose to stay at home with their children. Knowing that I had so much company in this new occupation was little comfort, as there were many days, particularly in the early stages, where I felt completely alone. Back then, I used to believe that by turning to motherhood as the primary role in my life, I thereby relinquished my identity as an independent thinker, contributor, and leader in society. Everyone would see me as "just a mom."

Initially, the biggest challenge for me was feeling like I was losing my identity. I had based a lot of my self-worth in my career. I liked everything about my job—relating to clients, seeing things change because of my ideas, using my creativity in different ways, being part of a team, having responsibility and the independence of earning my own money, and having structure in my day. I felt like I was an important contributor at work and in my community, and after ten years in the same career field, I was really starting to hit my stride.

Now in my thirties, I had the blend of experience and maturity with the energy of youth. I was long past the inexperience and awkwardness of my twenties, and I was earning a good living and doing what I loved. I was actively involved in professional clubs and organizations and often volunteered for additional work and responsibilities. Life was often stressful, but I thrived on it. I worked long hours, never making it to the gym before or after work like I planned. I was over-committed, over-stressed, and over-extended, and still, I loved it.

Urgency

Stephen Covey wrote a book titled *The Seven Habits of Highly Effective People*. In it, he discusses the comparison of "urgent versus important." Covey's book was not new when I read it, but it spoke to me in an entirely new way as I sat at my desk in a Dallas office building. It struck me that the phone calls, the line that was on hold, the "fax me this by close of business today," the "you've got mail," and the unplanned five o'clock meeting all felt urgent. Urgent was exhilarating. Urgent *seemed* important. But "urgent" was really *stress* that someone had created and then passed down to me. Generally speaking, most things I was working on could wait; someone along the line had just decided they couldn't. Much of my "urgent" work was either unnecessary or not critically important. At the very least, many projects I labored over, stressed over, and rushed to finish could have waited until later. They sure seemed desperately important in the moment, and I certainly never took the time to question just how critical they really were.

Obviously many jobs have critically important aspects to them that cannot wait or be delegated to others. But my job was not one of these. I needed a dose of perspective to be reminded that this job, project, or client was not the most important thing in my life.

What's Really Important

Many people believe that there is a higher cause and a greater good to our purposes in life. And though we all may have heard or thought it at one time, I suspect that many are like I was: never considering how that relates to your life, your family, and the decisions you make.

I had to reevaluate what my priorities were. Was I going to let the "tyranny of the urgent" dictate how I lived my life (Charles Hummel, *Tyranny of the Urgent* [Downers Grove, IL: Intervarsity Press, 1999])? How was I going to begin reordering the aspects of my career, family, and marriage to fit with what I knew deep down was important?

If my marriage and family truly were the valuable things to me, was I treating them as such?

Was I able to admit that I had allowed my career life to define and determine my path in life? Was I able to acknowledge that I had also failed to consider God's role in my life? Was I going to try to seek out what it is He wanted me to do? What was my real mission?

Life Lesson #4. It is crucial to be spiritually grounded.

There are many people who acknowledge there is a God yet do not make Him a part of any life decision. God is not on our radar and doesn't factor in. Many more may not be sure He exists, or if He does, they're not convinced that He's really all that concerned with what they're doing. Others believe that God can't be that invested in our hopes and dreams or more of them would come true. God must not be aware of our struggles or He'd be there to help us with the details of our lives. So, all too frequently there is emptiness in our lives—emptiness that God should and could occupy—that we instead fill with the busyness of our own pursuits. We dismiss God and the spiritual aspect of life and go about doing our own thing.

Ninety-two percent of Americans acknowledge a higher calling and a higher authority than just themselves, even if they don't necessarily equate it with God (Pew Religions Survey, http://religions.pewforum.org). Personally I think it's easier to be humble and grateful if you understand that someone else is responsible for the big things in life. Yet, it's important to understand that God is not just something or someone prompting us to do good things. I know Him as the God of the universe—the maker of everything—and I can be assured that He is bigger than I realize. My view and understanding are like yours, frequently limited to only what I have seen, heard, felt, and experienced. I'm convinced only a few of us have the full picture of God.

A Native American legend describes a giant tree standing in the forest. The bird on the branch sees a nice limb to perch on. The bear below sees a nice trunk to climb. The hawk above sees a nice view to soar above. The man sees a nice place to rest against. All of these observations are correct, yet each is only a small part of the overall tree. Each sees the tree for what it was to them.

God is like that. He is something different to everyone, and He has many characteristics that comprise Him. To describe Him by only one of those things, though, would be to miss all the parts and ultimately to misunderstand the whole. The idea of God will mean something different to everyone reading this. He may seem like a branch, or a trunk, or a shady place to rest against. But I would argue that He is all of these things...and more. He is also not just a God of one part of your life; He is relevant for all of it.

So, where does God fit?

I personally needed to be intentional about seeking God's will for everything: my career, my marriage, my family, and myself. I had to know Him before I could begin to know myself. I had to know His plan before I began to craft any plan of my own.

I knew that if I was unsure of where I stood with God, I would be at the mercy of the prevailing winds of contemporary culture. I had been there once and I learned cultural winds change a lot. Without a relationship with God, nothing would be grounding me that would be reliable and consistent. That would make life, and everything relating to it, really hard—certainly harder than it needs to be. I also knew that if I was unsure of what I believed about God, I would only pass that lack of belief and uncertainty on to any children I might have. And even when I was unmarried, I was uncomfortable that I didn't really have that part of my life nailed down.

I didn't like that I couldn't articulate my beliefs. It was unsettling. It was easier to stay away from church altogether than to be confronted with my inconsistencies and failures. But it continued to haunt me and caused me to lack contentment. Finding acceptance from friends and having fun were not difficult. Finding peace was.

A capstone, architecturally speaking, is the center point by which an arch itself holds together. Each of us has a capstone of belief by which our values hold together. It is what everything ties into. I try to make that capstone be my faith in God. The decisions I make are held together and framed by that relationship. I believe that if I live without a faith that is secure, I will be inconsistent in my choices and frequently motivated by the wrong things. I also believe that if we are unclear or uncertain about what we believe, we will pass that along to our kids as well in what we say as well as what we don't say.

Rich Nathan of Vineyard Columbus states, "Our choices have consequences. Wrong choices have dire consequences." The beliefs we put into our own personal worldview navigate the life we lead. If I conclude that God is irrelevant or unimportant, my choices and decisions will reflect that. If I conclude, as I do, that God is absolutely fundamental to all of life, then my choices and decisions should mirror that as well.

I can't begin to know where each reader is coming from in terms of their faith. Who or what you believe in, I have no idea. This is not a theology book. I can only speak to what I know and what I've experienced and how it relates to raising a family and setting life goals. I know that I had to settle in my mind and heart where I was in regard to God to make everything else fall into place.

My convictions are determined by my faith, and my decisions are determined by my convictions. This whole circular framework sets up the grid for my life. My faith anchors my marriage, it navigates how I raise my son, and it directs each choice I make. Where we stand on this couldn't be more important, since our faith and convictions are passed on to our children.

The Next Generation

Kids determine their faith early. By the age of eighteen, 90% of kids have already decided whether God is an important part of their lives or not. Only 13% of adults seek to make a change in their religious understanding (www.barna.org). When it comes to spiritual matters, what is taught in the home during childhood sticks.

If kids see hypocrisy in relation to what we say about our faith or how we live our lives, they will likely conclude that religion, any religion, is not for them. If they see that God is only a god of rules and restrictions who is unyielding, unbending, and intolerant, they will never take the time to learn who God truly is. If they only see a family of Easter Sundays and Christmas concerts, they will put God in the same category as the Easter Bunny and Santa Claus, something of a mythical creature that, although comforting, is unrelated to their lives outside the walls of the church.

*Our kids learn that we value God, or they learn that
we value something else.*

When God becomes the most important thing in your life, your perspective changes because it transforms you. Looking back now, much of what I, as a career woman, felt was urgent, pressing, and necessary was really fueled by an incessant need to please, selfishness, greed, pride, or, frankly, just a need to feel useful or busy. It was also stoked by my lack of perspective and priority.

I certainly didn't maintain the bigger picture. I was too busy chasing the thing in front of me to see the road out ahead and where it was really leading me. And by keeping my sights so short, I missed out on a lot. I cheated myself and my relationships.

I turned so inward that I forgot how much my decisions and actions affected others. I spent years of my life missing out on what God had planned for me to do.

And I never meant for it to happen; it just did. No one sat me down and told me otherwise, or maybe they tried to and I just didn't listen. Even if I did listen, I certainly didn't respond. I'm sure people saw a lack of perspective in me, but most were too polite to say anything. But make no mistake about it, there was a time when my needs and wants were seriously mixed up. I was inwardly focused, trying hard to measure up, knocking myself out attempting to gain the respect of others and trying to do something significant...but only through my work.

I sincerely believe it all boiled down to perspective and ultimately my understanding of where I stood with God. Though I had been raised in the church and was a believer early on, I still saw God as being there when you really needed him but distantly involved, generally disinterested, and fairly hard to please. I also thought once I disappointed God, by messing up, that was it. I was on the "outs" with Him, and I could no longer enjoy His favor, attention, or love.

But I learned that He wasn't really like I thought He was, and I was able to learn who He was for real. It was quite a surprise. There's a lot to God. He is worth careful consideration. He is also worth trusting, praying to, and getting to know. The God I worship is a loving God and is alive and active in the world. He is intrinsically involved in our lives, whether we acknowledge Him or even want Him to be. He is a God of relevance in our day, in this culture, and in our lives. Once I got my relationship with God figured out, the rest of my life fell into place. I'm convinced that He was, and still is, the key.

Life Lesson #5. How to make tough moral choices.

In resting on the principles of faith, the perimeters of life become clear because there is a moral framework in which to operate. The big issues like honesty, morality, forgiveness, self-control, and anger (just to name a few) are now viewed through the lens of the faith that you claim. The Bible explains this quite well: "So I say, live by the Spirit, and you will not gratify the desires of the sinful nature. For the sinful nature desires what is contrary to the Spirit, and the Spirit what is contrary to the sinful nature. They are in conflict with each other, so that you do not do what you want" (Galatians 5:16-17).

I want to help my son know what to rely on when he's standing alone and faced with a difficult moral choice. I want my son to know how to respond when he is surrounded by others who are tempting him to compromise his character.

Importance

Clearly, our roles as parents fall into the *important* category. I had to remind myself that *my life* was not *my work*. None of us should be defined by our work. Our job in the workplace, no matter how lucrative or highly respected, is just an extension of our abilities and gifts; it should never define us.

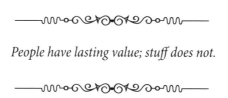

People have lasting value; stuff does not.

And this is not news to anyone reading this. Yet, we live as if we don't know this is true. As a modern society, we continue to invest in that which does not last to gain that which we cannot keep, while largely dismissing that which is lasting and vital. We say one thing and do another.

We say we have our priorities lined up, but our checkbooks and calendars don't agree.

Consistently Inconsistent

Recently I was amused by the drink order of a young woman at Starbucks. While careful to specify that she wanted no caffeine, no sugar, and no milkfat in her coffee drink, she was quick to remind the barista that she wanted the whipped cream and caramel sauce on top. Some people know this as the "double cheeseburger and a diet Coke" mentality.

So it is with much of what we say we believe. We say certain things, we believe certain things, but we often fail to see that our lives are not being lived out consistently with our words and beliefs.

If we say we really want to impact our families and bring up our children in the best possible environment, some of us may need to weigh the impact we have in our current job against the value of our children and the lasting impact we each can have on our families.

When I think of my best memories, they are experiences with emotional strings attached. They are times that someone spent with me, the way someone made me feel, the times I persevered when the going got tough, and the times I was challenged, joyful, or grieving. For as great as some of the days in my career were, I can't remember the specifics of any deal I made. What I remember are the friendships and relationships I made. I remember when I volunteered for community service events and when I went beyond the call to help someone. My memories now are filled with snippets of lunchtime conversations, office practical jokes, and the times I laughed, learned, and cried. I now do not look back on work as anything more than that.

One of my favorite movies is *About Schmidt*, a movie starring Jack Nicholson. It is a story about a retired Nebraska insurance executive who finds out, after retirement, what life is truly all about. One of the most moving scenes is when he revisits his old office, merely days after his retirement of over thirty years, to find that the man replacing him has no time or interest in anything that he did while he was there. Schmidt finds the files he was so careful to maintain thrown in the dumpster. The life he was so set on defining himself by was so easily replicated. At the end of the movie, it is something and someone altogether different that give his life meaning. It's a good reminder that we simply cannot give ourselves fully, heart, mind, and soul, to our career identity; it doesn't mean anything in the end.

Dorothy, We're Not in Kansas Anymore

I grew up in Kansas. Not many people, I've learned over the years, have ever really been to Kansas. Most have flown over or driven through it on their way to somewhere else. Since I'm from there, I get the usual *Wizard of Oz* comments, and nearly everyone asks me if I've seen a tornado. I've never seen an actual tornado, but I've seen what one can do.

In April 1991, a tornado cut a path of destruction through Andover, Kansas, a bedroom community of Wichita, and left little in its wake. Hundreds of homes were destroyed and the community was mobilized to assist those who had been affected.

As an employee of one of the local television stations, I was sent out with one of the many Red Cross disaster teams. I saw foundations of houses that were swept away. I saw cars destroyed and people wandering around shocked and dazed, losing everything they had in only a few minutes. I remember seeing furniture scattered about and personal items heaped in piles of debris. But the image I remember most vividly is a fence line with items attached to each post. One post had a boot, another a shirt, yet another a lampshade. The fence stretched out for miles, as far as the eye could see, with items of every imaginable type tethered to the posts. The fence was still in place, but everything else had blown away. No one had placed those items; they were simply caught up in the storm and deposited wherever they fell.

Back then, I looked at my career like that fence. It provided me a secure sense of identity and purpose. Everything else in my life might change or go away, but I always had my career. Thinking of giving it up was scary. I didn't know what my fence was going to be anymore. I was afraid I would lose my identity if I didn't work. I would be hidden away in a house somewhere in this new parenting role, a role that I was ill-prepared for and where there would be no accolades, appreciation, or identity. I feared I would be forgotten to everyone but my family and closest friends, and that even they would find me less interesting and easier to forget over time.

God gave us important work to do as parents. It is arguably the most valuable work most of us will ever do. Spending important years as a stay-at-home parent can be a richly textured experience built upon the framework that you developed while you were in the workplace. Many of the skills used in your career can transfer to the stay-at-home experience. Even without a paycheck, we are still bright, effective, efficient, and enterprising people who need to give our families the very best we have to offer.

I feel we stand in a unique position. We have a different perspective than those who are not career oriented or chose different paths. We're also different than those who remain in the career field with or without the responsibility of a family. Most career women bring a different set of expectations, hopes, and experiences to the parenting experience.

Once we acknowledge that we are wonderful, creative, interesting, and complex people, whether we are carrying a briefcase or a diaper bag, then our journey can begin. We can use many of the characteristics that made us good at our jobs to make us good at parenting. We set our own agenda. God has given us a powerful and unique position within our families and communities, and it's ours to embrace.

Parents who place a high priority on their families are proven to have a greater impact on their families and their communities (www.msnbc.com). Having a parent at home really does change the dynamics of the household. Research has shown that children without a parent at home are less likely to eat well and exercise and spend more time in front of the television or computer than those who have at least one parent at home. The employment of mothers, in particular, often has a negative effect on the educational attainment of their children. And children handle the absence of parents differently. A recent study shows that full-time maternal employment negatively affects boys academically more than girls. And interestingly, mothers who work full time tend to raise daughters who do the same (www. sciencedirect.com).

We should be confident in knowing that our role at home is very important indeed, and we should never feel the need to prove ourselves by what the culture sets up as the standard. Children have a better chance of receiving the time and emotional support they will need to nurture their development if there is a parent at home. Working spouses can be supported and encouraged as well, their effectiveness in the workplace increased, and their self-esteem bolstered. Working partners can be freed from many of the distractions that channel energy away from doing what they need to do as leaders of the home, workplace, church, and community.

As the parent at home, we also have the opportunity to listen to our hearts. We can make more time to care for our loved ones. We can make more time to enrich our friendships with others. We can explore our dreams and rediscover ourselves. And we can be the fulcrum maintaining the delicate balance of family and life's demands.

Being a parent who is present is an awesome journey. When I stepped outside the busyness and pressure of the work world, I learned much about myself. I began to create meaningful change in myself, my family, and the world around me. I found value and meaning in my God-given gifts and was able to learn how best to use them.

Life Lesson #6. Seek to find balance in life.

In 2009, I watched an interview of people out of work due to the economic downturn who were surprised that they lost weight, learned to sleep through the night for the first time in years, reconnected with hobbies and friends, and learned a lot about themselves. Time away from work can often be healing, and unexpectedly enjoyable, even when the circumstances are not of our choosing.

Finding out what you love to do may seem obvious, but the challenge is figuring out how to make whatever it is fit appropriately into our lives. Some might think that to do what we love is to abandon all sense of responsibility and follow dreams wherever they lead us. And though following dreams is something I support, I also know that there are stark realities that factor in. I may have had a dream to be a professional tennis player or a concert pianist. But I didn't have the inherent talent, begin early enough in life, or have the adequate training. It wasn't what God had planned for me.

Do I give up tennis or piano, or anything else, simply because I cannot do them as fully as I would have dreamed? Or can I incorporate them into parts of my life in ways that are both beneficial and balanced?

I want my son to find and do what brings him joy, even if it doesn't lead to fame or professional success. The things that he loves to do will help make the things he doesn't love to do sustainable. We all often must do what we don't want to in order for work to be done or progress to be made. Yet, inside all of us is a need to do the things we love in order to recreate, relax, or express ourselves creatively. These things bring us balance and help our lives to be sustainable.

I want my son Kasey to appreciate the gifts God has given him and use them throughout his life, actively looking for ways to serve, teach, and lead by using those gifts.

Too many of us stop doing what brings us joy and only do what we feel we have to. I believe there is a balance between our responsibilities and routine, and our sense of fun and fulfillment.

I think we know in our heart what our gifts are. They make us unique and give us joy. My abilities to write, to be athletic, and to encourage others aren't things I struggle with. They are part of who I am at the very core, the package God gave me. I have often wanted to be more than I am, or different than I am, but at the end of the day, I am uniquely me.

I've learned that I love being a mom. Motherhood has been an incredible, surprising, and fulfilling experience. It uses all the gifts I've been given in ways I never would have expected. Being a mom brings me joy because through it I am able to integrate my gifts with those I impact most and direct my gifts toward those I love most.

If we each find our value in who we are according to God's standard and design, not by our salary, professional title, or contribution within the workplace, we are poised to be our most successful. I don't need accolades in places of power and prestige. "You're awesome, Mom," is all I ever really need to hear.

"There are different kinds of gifts, but the same Spirit. There are different kinds of service, but the same Lord. There are different kinds of working, but the same God works all of them in all men."

~ 1 Corinthians 12:4–6

Chapter 4
A New Beginning

"Though no one can go back and make a brand new start, anyone can start from now and make a brand new ending."
~ Carl Bard

B eginning something is usually easy. I've started many a New Year's resolution, book, or project, but stepping into this new arena of readjusting and reordering my life didn't seem easy at all.

I had physically made the step away from the career world. Yet, I felt unprepared for the challenges ahead of me and a bit overwhelmed. I had never done anything like this before, and now that I had, I was dogged with questions. And, as I would later learn, the answers would be slow in coming.

What were the logistics of beginning a life at home?

What would an average day look like?

What was reasonable to expect in terms of measuring goals?

How would I know if I was successful in this new position?

I knew I would need to get some kind of action plan together or I would feel completely out of sorts. Those first weeks, all I did was respond to the immediate tasks at hand, and with an infant, that varied little. Feeding, changing, feeding, changing, nap. Repeat.

A lack of focus and direction is not uncommon for anyone in the midst of a transition. Reacting to the most pressing need in front of us may be all we can do. When my son was a baby, my biggest goals usually were simply to get in a shower and make dinner. Somehow the hours between morning and evening just disappeared.

Baby, What a Day!

There are many seasons in our parenting life, and each one is remarkably short. I think that infancy has to be the toughest and shortest season of all. Babies only stay babies for what seems like an instant. As soon as they are rolling over, pushing up, sitting up, and then walking, we may still call them babies but they are much more than that—toddling, inquiring, watching, learning, and discovering. What you gain in their budding independence it seems you lose in your own. It's "all hands on deck" at that point, and you might feel that you're losing any control you might have had.

But as life with this new little one calms down and you find your way within this new stage of life, you may wonder just how you're going to formulate this working plan for yourself and your family. All that you've read so far sounds good, but just how are you going to go about it? And what if your kids are already in school? Does that make the decision to stay home any less significant or any easier?

For some of us, the decision to take on full-time parenting happens after the kids are past the point of diapers and teething.

I don't believe it matters at what point we stop and consider the decision to take on full-time parenting—just that we do.

It's never too late to jump in and experience the joy of the journey. Kids, regardless of their age, desire for their parents to be present for them. I don't think we're less needed once they start school and it's quite possible we are needed more.

After working for years, you shouldn't feel the need to start some new agenda the very first day, week, or even month. It may be that a bit of a break is well deserved. Enjoy this time of transition and allow yourself to readjust. A little period of no direction and no particular plan can be quite rejuvenating.

But obviously you can't stay there. Soon it will start to hit you that everything has been turned upside down, and you may begin to miss the purposefulness of work and the interaction of coworkers, or simply wonder how things "back at the office" are going. If you're like me, you'll feel the urge to call and check in with everyone. That's okay, since it's natural to miss your friends and wonder how your clients or coworkers are doing. With that in mind, here are a few steps to take to ease the transition from full-time career professional to full-time career parent.

I found that this was the perfect time to start setting up my work space at home. It need not be an entire room, perhaps just an area set aside on the kitchen counter or table. It doesn't really matter as long as it's your space. Equip it with items you will need to begin your new position.

It might seem silly to discuss setting up a workspace for someone who is no longer in an office setting. Yet, I think we often don't consider that we are setting ourselves up in an entirely new occupation at home. Organization is key to success in anything we do, and this is no exception. Part of the role you will take on involves family management, which has heavy social and financial planning aspects. I run my life out of what my husband calls "Mommy Central." It is only a space on a countertop in the kitchen near the phone, but it is where everything begins and ends at our house. In the drawer and cabinet below are the things I use most often. Everything I use regularly is within easy reach.

I think this is important, for it demarcates your own space. For me, it helped encapsulate, in a physical sense, that this was a new career. Even now, I think of my husband as the family's chairman of the board and myself as the family's CEO, head of finance, operations, and public relations, custodian, psychologist, chef, and nurse. My role varies from day to day, hour to hour, and sometimes minute to minute. It is part of the challenge of this new career. It is never boring, and it requires discipline and a tremendous breadth of ability. Talk about multi-tasking...this is it!

I've often thought that if stay-at-home-moms created a resume after their years of staying home, there would be very few positions for which they wouldn't qualify or have some working knowledge.

Many mothers have actually listed on resumes the responsibilities they had while taking time off from their careers. More than a fancy job title, employers are interested in the marketable skills you bring to a job. I'm convinced that by learning to manage and lead our households in a purposeful way, we're not hurting our future career opportunities.

Part of my adjustment process included learning to embrace this new future. It also meant that I could not romanticize my old job, remembering it as being more glamorous, fun, or important than it really was.

Embracing the future didn't mean holding on to the past too tightly. If I continued to believe I wouldn't be able to handle this, in the physical or emotional sense, I probably wouldn't. I've learned to be a believer in the power of the mind, and I'm convinced that we must begin each new chapter in our lives with confidence, and a belief in our instincts.

Training for and running marathons taught me a lot about what self-confidence can do and what happens when you dare to do something you may have previously considered impossible.

I've run two of them, and I describe the experience as 26.2 miles of character building. Marathon running is something I never imagined I'd ever do or want to do. I didn't even start running until age thirty. Even now, years later, I can't believe I participated in anything requiring such stamina and discipline. But, as in so many things, the longest journey starts with the smallest step.

I'm not a fast runner. I would be called an average or a middle-to back-of-the-pack runner. It doesn't come as easily to me as other things, and though long-distance running can be immensely enjoyable, it can also be brutal.

The marathon requires disciplined training and dedication. You don't decide the day of a marathon that you're going to run one; you plan for weeks, sometimes months in advance. Medals only go to the finishers, and knowing that was enough motivation for me. I didn't just want to say I entered a marathon; I wanted to say I completed one. I wanted the medal and to know that I did what I set out to do.

But I learned that the key to success—despite the training, regardless of the venue, and with or without the latest shoes, tech gear, or diet—is will and attitude. It's true that you must put in the necessary training time and effort, but believing that you *can* do it and that you have it within you to accomplish it will be what gets you over the finish line. The power of those on the sidelines cheering you on is also invaluable.

At mile twenty of my first marathon, when I was really starting to hurt, another runner patted me on the back. It was a seventy-three-year-old gentleman, on his way to completing his twelfth marathon. He came up behind me, and with a "way to go sweetie," proceeded to run with me for a couple of miles. Then he politely excused himself and passed me. But he was there at the finish line, giving me the thumbs-up as I got wrapped in my foil blanket. He'll never know what a boost to my confidence he gave me that day. Similarly, we can gain parenting strength and confidence from other parents around us as well as support and encourage others in differing stages of the journey. We are not alone, and we all share common ground when it comes to raising our children the best we can.

A small but I think important change you may have to make during this transition has to do with your wardrobe. While this may sound obvious to many of you, it wasn't to me. I assembled the clothes, shoes, and accessories from my working days, boxed them, and moved them out of my closet and into storage. They just didn't fit my life anymore. It seemed to make more sense to simplify and streamline.

I assembled a new work wardrobe. But just what did that consist of? What made sense for the job I was about to take on?

Of course, from a practical standpoint you can wear whatever you want, from sweatpants to designer labels, but I think that it's important to set a standard of dressing.

I feel it is important to put myself together each day because I believe that there is a connection between how we look and how we feel.

I can sense it in myself, and I can see it in others.

Every woman has her own style. You can figure that out on your own. But I will make the appeal for you to be modest and appropriate. Dress your age and dress for the role you play. Don't feel you can't have style just because you're not in an office anymore, and don't worry about having the latest look if that isn't your thing.

One idea is to pick and buy things that are neat looking even after a full day: washable, not dry-clean only, comfortable, and not particularly expensive. On any given day I can be showered, dressed, and out the door in thirty minutes. And though I continue to put effort into how I look, I don't obsess. I try to make every effort to look neat yet be functional. I know I am a professional with important work to do, so I want to strike a balance between feeling good about my appearance and using my time wisely.

Remembering that our outer appearances are not what make us special. Our inner closet is what we should fill with beautiful things.

I take inspiration from the biblical description of "a wife of noble character," taken from Proverbs 31: "She is worth far more than rubies. Her husband has full confidence in her and lacks nothing of value....She sets about her work vigorously; her arms are strong for her tasks....She is clothed with strength and dignity; she can laugh at the days to come. She speaks with wisdom, and faithful instruction is on her tongue. She watches over the affairs of her household and does not eat the bread of idleness. Her children arise and call her blessed; her husband also, and he praises her."

The woman here is described by her work ethic, inner strength, faith, and wisdom, not by the clothes she wears. So, most importantly clothe yourselves with kindness, wisdom, and truth, and you'll know you'll be dressed just right.

Life Lesson #7. The value of hard work and discipline.

I can tell my son to work hard in academics, physical labor, or athletics, yet he won't truly understand the concepts of hard work and discipline unless he's seen them exemplified by others around him and been placed into situations himself that require it. He also won't fully grasp it unless he's seen it lived out in our own home, in everyday circumstances and situations. By learning to work hard himself, he will then appreciate and value the hard work of others. He will understand that nothing important gets accomplished without it.

At age fourteen, my son is not seeking to add responsibility to his life if it requires actual "work." He loves the newfound freedoms that comes with age and independence but has a natural resistance to anything that takes time away from doing what he wants to do.

Taking the time to instruct him on how to mow the lawn, for example, is necessary for him to have the skill to do it himself, but it also requires patience, trial and error, and practice. Sure, it would be easier to do it ourselves, to hire it done, or to pass a job off as unimportant or not expected given his school schedule or sports commitments. But mowing the lawn teaches him more than just how to cut grass. It teaches him that there is responsibility involved in owning a home and that some things need to be completed and are part of being in a family. We are also granting him a privilege by trusting him with an important job, teaching him the beauty of a job well done, and showing him the honor and joy of honest labor.

Those principles will serve him well for years to come.

Chapter 5
New Expectations

"Action springs not from thought,
but from a readiness for responsibility."
~ Dietrich Bonhoeffer

In my first few weeks of time at home, I got frustrated that I wasn't accomplishing as much as I had expected. I had left this great career and was feeling like a mediocre new mother. Being a new mom was special, but it was a lot to take on. I missed the structure of my work life. I did my best to plan the day around my new responsibilities, workouts, feedings, and nap times. Yet, everything I did seemed random and reactive. I felt inadequate, overwhelmed, frumpy, and tired.

I didn't think I was trying to have it all. I just wanted
some affirmation that I was on the right track.

And yes, I wanted to fit back in my old jeans...and yes, I wanted to have a perfectly planned meal for dinner every night...and yes, I wanted my son to nap at the same time every day...and yes, I hoped to be able to find time for me.

Okay, I wanted it all, and I wanted it all *now*!

I think the post–baby boom generation was the first to assume we could have it all at the same time: career, home, personal life—the whole package. I'm quite sure my mother never entertained the idea that she could work outside the home, raise a family, and do all the things I try to do. So, without giving up something where did we get this crazy idea that we, as this evolved generation of women, could expect to accomplish what no other women before us had ever done?

We demand so much from ourselves and often continue adding things to our lives without ever taking anything away, forgetting that life is a balance and that there are only so many hours in a day.

I'm as guilty of this as anyone. I have always been driven to do more and have often overextended myself at the expense of others.

I am constantly challenged to slow down and spend time with people instead of rushing to accomplish one more task. I sometimes am annoyed by unplanned phone calls or events that take up precious time in my day. I often hesitate to reach out to others because I'm so focused on getting my own agenda accomplished. So, clearly, I can be selfish with my time, and I am not immune to the overachieving syndrome that is so pervasive in our culture.

Years ago many of us went off to college or graduate school and then into the workforce, fully anticipating and expecting to have it all: career, family, great marriage, and a totally fulfilled life. Somewhere along the line we adopted the idea that there was a way to have everything. We may have even considered that the role our mothers played was outdated—noble, but out of touch. With our education and our enlightened attitude, we could squeeze all the juice out of life and pave the way for future generations.

I believe the women who went before us were more comfortable with their roles in the world. They weren't called "household manager" or "stay-at-home mom," they were simply "mother" and "wife." That was enough for them, for society, and for everyone. No one questioned the validity of what they did, and no one considered their vocation anything but honorable. When I was growing up, it was the women that *did* work outside the home that were often made to feel different, although even by then, there were more of them in the workplace than ever. Now we have a misalignment of expectations in regard to the parental roles: moms expect to do everything and do it well without considering that often something is lost along the way.

It is amazing that expectations and experience should change so much in such a short time. Grandmothers I have talked to have told me they didn't worry as much as mothers do today. They explained how many women didn't go to college, married younger, started their families right away, and did what they thought was right, within the norms of the day.

A Different Day Has Dawned

Undoubtedly we are living in a different time now, but the role of parent remains an important one. Certainly, we look at it in different ways than we did in 1970. That we went on to further our education and then delve into careers makes us look at parenting and how we arrange our lives in other ways.

Every mother has come to her own decision whether to work or not work outside the home, and she should be comfortable with that decision. Each family has to evaluate their priorities and how they will pursue their own goals. And whatever decision is made, it should be made together as a family. I feel strongly that being home with your kids is the best choice, even though it can often be a difficult one to make.

A Unique Calling

Certainly coming from the work arena does not make us *more* qualified but it does make us *uniquely* qualified and, I think, well prepared for the role of stay-at-home parent. As professionals from the workplace, we can blend elements of a more traditional stay-at-home role with the education, experience, and enterprise our working days afforded us. We bring a variety of different skills and experiences to the table and can make intelligent and informed choices about how our family operates. Without the structure of a traditional work setting, we can experience more flexibility in our day and use our creativity with a newly directed sense of purpose. We are poised to be parents who can lead our families to real and authentic success.

Success vs. Significance Revisited

Back in the 1990s, there was a lot of talk about *success* versus *significance*. Even then, it was not a new idea, but decades later it's still an important one. I feel it is key, especially for professional women, that we remember the difference between what the world views as "success" and what is truly "significant." Making the choice to stay home with your family may not show results that can be quantified or measured until much later down the road.

The investment made now is all part of a long-term strategy.

Consider the Chinese bamboo tree. Over the course of four years it is planted, watered, cultivated, and nurtured, with not so much as a shoot emerging from the ground to show for it. Farmers must continue to work the fields and trust and wait while the seed is being formed. On the fifth year a shoot can finally be seen. At that point, the bamboo rockets toward the sky at an alarming rate, sometimes as tall as eighty feet.

So it seems with our kids. We invest in them for years—tending, nurturing, caring for, and feeding them—until one day they are able to make their own choices and lead their own lives. It is then we truly see the investment made so long ago. Did we raise them with self-esteem? Did we teach them to seek truth? Did we love them unconditionally and help them make wise choices? We will surely see all of this play out at some point, and then we will know.

Our ideas of successful parenting are also wrapped up in all kinds of expectations. Very likely, the more success you achieved in your career, the greater the expectations you bring to this new staying-at-home role. The stakes are high in this new job and the desire to succeed can sometimes overwhelm us.

Some assume that to raise a child in the best way involves highly paid or highly trained childcare workers and educators. Many are convinced that a prestigious academy or highly popular daycare is better than what they would be able to offer at home.

"I just wouldn't be any good at it," one mother of an early elementary student told me. "It would feel like a waste of my talents. I'm not a patient person. I'd get bored. I wouldn't know what to do with her all day. At daycare, she gets to interact with other children and do crafts and art projects. She loves it. She doesn't even want to leave when I pick her up in the afternoon. Besides, I feel we do get quality time together...in the evenings."

This mom was just being honest. This is how she really saw things. The challenge is to avoid masking our true feelings with reasoning and justification. Maybe you've even felt the way this mother felt or have known friends or coworkers who have. And it's true that there are many childcare facilities staffed with loving, highly trained, passionate professionals. But despite any impressive-sounding name, the credentials of the employees, or the appealing and attractive facility, the reality is that each of those children are not with their parents and are not being primarily trained and nurtured in the unique environment only a parent can offer.

"Fewer things with more life" needs to be our new attitude. The new cars, big houses, and fancy vacations are fine, unless they are ultimately keeping us from experiencing time with our kids. Our time on this earth is remarkably brief, and days, weeks, and years can fly by before we stop to ask whether our time is well spent.

Working parents are obviously not bad parents; they are simply stretched very, very thin. Statistics say that working parents spend 80% of their day not directly relating to their kids. Sleeping, school and daycare hours, commuting, and eating/bathing/dressing time mean the average family spends no more than three hours a day together. When parents or kids spend time regularly in non-communicative activities, such as watching television, internet activity, or gaming, that time is reduced to just over an hour a day. That means there is only an hour a day to relate, bond, teach, nurture, encourage, and play together. An hour a day to discover each other and become the family you want to be. That's a lot of pressure on one hour.

Research shows that our work, in and of itself, is not the most important variable influencing our children's positive development. Instead, it is the mother's attitude and acceptance with her choice to work, and the general warmth, sensitivity, and responsiveness she shows to her kids. When asked how kids felt about their parents working, the majority responded that they didn't really care one way or the other. They simply wanted to see their parents less stressed and tired. They wished the time they spent with their parents was unrushed, focused, and calm. Many have found that serving dual careers is not only stressful but potentially fruitless. By the time all of the resulting expenses are considered, many second incomes do not garner enough money to logically justify the effort:

"The Two-Income Trap is thick with irony. Middle-class mothers went into the workforce in a calculated effort to give their families an economic edge. Instead, millions of them are now in the workplace just so their families can break even. When mothers joined the workforce, the family gave up something of considerable (although unrecognized) economic value: an extra skilled and dedicated adult, available to pitch in to help save the family" (www.familiesandwork.org).

Our checkbooks and calendars prove what our priorities are.

I think everyone would agree that our greatest and most valuable asset is undoubtedly our time. All around us are amazing innovations and electronics designed to give us more time. We are in a big hurry, and we are not patient people. New technology over the last several years has transformed us into an instant-gratification generation. We are constantly in search of ways to get more hours out of our day so that we can do what is important and enjoyable. Technology has made efficiency possible in ways never seen before, yet we've managed to fill much of that extra time with the expectations of getting *even more* done. We are working more hours than ever, and sleeping fewer hours than ever. Meanwhile, statistics show that despite all of the technological advances, families are spending less time together.

The Toll "No Time" Takes on Families

Divorce affects over a third of parents today. Although the divorce rate has leveled off in recent years, it nevertheless is a decision many of us make at some point in our parenting lives.

"Divorce may be the right decision, but you worry about the impact on your children. Studies show that children from divorced families have an increased likelihood of depression, substance abuse, and trust issues. But these outcomes are not written in stone," says psychologist Christy Buchanan, PhD. "The degree of difficulty children experience depends on their parents' behavior" (www.workingmother.com).

Single-parent families can have strong foundations that continue to strengthen through adversity. There are families that have one parent that travels for work and the other parent takes total responsibility. It is all about priorities, how we balance our time, and what matters most.

In the United States, we often choose to trade time with our kids for vocational productivity and professional success, partly because materialism and competitiveness are so deeply ingrained in our American lifestyle. We are certainly not the only country that struggles with balancing materialism and life, but as Americans, we are among the wealthiest people on the planet. The fact that we have clean drinking water, a place to sleep, and clothes to wear puts us in a very small minority worldwide. Yet, it's not enough (Richard Stearns, *The Hole in the Gospel* [Nashville, TN: Thomas Nelson, 2009]). The United States is the only one of the world's high-income countries that continues to add to the number of average work hours per week. In Japan and Europe, the amount of hours has been on the decline. The United States also trails the rest of the world in amount of time off provided to working parents when a child is born (www.sharedprosperity.org/bp189.html).

We are having fewer children than previous generations, and we're spending less time with the ones we do have.

And while some may blame the media for tempting us with all that we could have, or suggesting all that we should have, we have no one to blame but ourselves. Regardless of the messages we hear or the marketing we are exposed to, it is deeply wired within the human psyche to want more. As Americans, we have just accepted it as the normal and preferable way of life.

Life Lesson #8. The true value of money.

For most people money represents far more than just the means to live or pay the bills. Money equals freedom, control, pleasure, security, and self-worth. The things money can buy are often just components of that same understanding. I want my son to understand that money is just a means to an end—currency for helping him do what he needs to do and not an identifying factor in who he is. Money doesn't make him smarter, more capable, or more likely to succeed.

I don't want money to be the reason he picks a certain school or profession. I also don't want the lack of money to keep him from pursuing his dreams. I want him to see that money can be both a blessing and a burden and that it needs to be handled with the understanding that it is not his to keep; its purpose is not solely to make life easier, and he should never compromise his integrity for the desire of it.

We've seen a changing of culture in recent times as the economy has risen and fallen. Many have been forced into reevaluating their job situation and recalculating perceived needs and wants. Leaner times give us an opportunity to evaluate what is most important to us. Sometimes life forces our hand. We may not have considered a different view of success until we were laid off, let go, or downsized. Now, we have to adjust our living, and we find over time that we really can do with so much less. We can find peace in the midst of the craziness, and we can reconnect with the basic elements of friends, family, and faith.

Just like the rest of America, after receiving the news of the attack on the World Trade Towers on that bright, sunny morning of September 11, 2001, I wasn't thinking about anything but those I loved—my husband, son, family, and friends.

I daresay no one that day was thinking about anything except the people they loved, cherished, and cared for most. The whole world seemed to draw in to family, faith, and friends for those weeks following the attack. Sadly, over time we lost that sense of closeness, and we resumed our lives in an altered but newly normative state.

We traveled again, we got lost in work again, and we stopped going to church again. But for those few brief days, everything felt different, because it was.

I think it's far too easy for us to lose sight of what is most precious to us and allow the business of life to drive our day and ultimately our life. It may be said that it takes a village to raise a child, but it doesn't need to. By recognizing the contributing factor we are individually in our kids' lives, we can step up in a big way to our role as parent and leader of our homes.

"'For I know the plans I have for you,' declares the Lord, 'plans to prosper you and not to harm you, plans to give you hope and a future. Then you will call on me and come and pray to me, and I will listen to you. You will seek me and find me when you seek me with all your heart. I will be found by you,' declares the Lord."

~ Jeremiah 29:11–14a

Strive to Be Your Own Person

I don't really know of anyone, once given a mission and convinced of their vital role in it, who doesn't tackle it with all they've got. Usually, you need to get out of their way. But often parents are navigating their way through parenting with no real mission and drifting around day by day with little direction.

Sailing is one of my newest interests. I'm fascinated by the way you can guide a boat in the water using nothing but the wind. Sailing looks easy, but it is really quite technical. Without proper use of the sail, control of the rudder, and an understanding of wind speed, water depth, and other conditions, you are simply left to drift wherever the wind takes you. And if the wind is directing you and you have no intervention, chances are you will end up either flipping the boat or getting stuck. Sailing also looks peaceful and serene from a distance, and it can be, but sailing is an active sport. It's very hands on. You don't just get into a sailboat and expect to go somewhere without putting in effort. Someone has to be controlling the rudder all the time, and though the ride is often enjoyable, a sailor can never be unaware of the conditions around him. So it is with parenting. Families left without someone at the helm are left to drift or capsize.

In shipbuilding, the term "laying the keel" refers to setting the hull or base of the ship during construction. It is the most significant part of the building process and is often celebrated with a dedication ceremony. Making the decision to lead our families in a goal-oriented manner is like this. We as parents can set the foundations for the ship of our families and then begin steering toward the destinations and goals we decide on. We should all lay the keel in our families.

We all need a plan, mission, and purpose or life feels meaningless.

By keeping our goals front and center, we are able to keep our families sailing in the right direction.

By keeping God front and center, we are given the wisdom, encouragement, security, and confidence that we need to lead our families through a challenging culture and time.

John Shinn, pastor of Calvary Baptist Church, Canton, Michigan used an acrostic for the word FIRST that helps me remember the things I should be considering on a regular basis.

*F*inances: Being a good steward of the financial blessings I have been given and being content with what I have.

*I*nterests: Seeking and maintaining activities that are healthy and nourish my role as a family leader.

*R*elationships: Investing in relationships that exhibit love and support, and seeking opportunities to reach out and love others.

*S*chedule: Making my family, marriage, and faith priorities in my life. Nothing speaks commitment more than the way I use my valuable time.

*T*alents: Using the talents and gifts God has uniquely given me to honor Him and my family.

I have to regularly make a habit of seeking the Lord's guidance and intervention. I find that without Him, I don't hold it together, stay focused, or find the joy in what I'm doing. It is God who allows me to live in the moment, like the day my son wanted to take the long way home from the park and pick up acorns when I was tired and eager to get home. It is God who has taught me to recognize the power of my words of encouragement as well as my words of criticism. It is God who guides me through the times I feel unappreciated, when He gently reminds me how many times I haven't appreciated Him.

Putting God first makes life less complicated and more joyful. More important, it keeps the focus on what really matters.

There has never been a more important time to seek God's guidance or His will for your life than now, as the parent. In this key leadership role, we are setting the course for a generation, as everything begins in the home. Children model what they see. You shape what they think and often how they react. What they consider important is likely what you have taught them to value. Being a parent and person of significance starts with you and your conviction and boldness to make your home, your children, and yourself different. That's real and authentic success defined.

Leslie is a married mother of three with a law degree from a well-respected university. Years ago, when her sons' school was without a headmaster, she voluntarily stepped into that role, took no pay, and continued to work diligently at it during a nearly two-year interim period. She's a great cook, plays the piano, is well read, and is completely dedicated. She's tall, smart, and pretty, and has always looked like Supermom to me.

Although she and I rarely see each other because we live so far away, she continues to inspire me. What attracted me to her is that she has always been so comfortable in her own skin. Clearly she could be out in the marketplace doing amazing things, earning accolades, prestige, and significant financial benefit. Yet, early on, she chose to make her family a priority and has never looked back. She is as professional at parenting as she ever was at the practice of law, and there is a beauty in her spirit that can be seen by all around her. I think that people who are doing what they were born to do are beautiful things to observe. I can't compare myself to her, because her gifts are different than mine, but she has remained an inspiration.

My husband is an amazing and inspiring person in his own right. Years ago, Ken was a very talented triathlete. He said that the key to his constant improvement in triathlons was that he consistently ran in training with a better runner, biked with a better biker, and swam with a better swimmer. To me, it always sounded like it would be hard on one's ego, but he recognized that by training in that way he improved in all three sports. I'm not sure he ever beat the better biker, outran the better runner, or outswam the better swimmer, but he improved his performance in three different events. He was confident enough to learn from those around him without constantly comparing himself to them.

I look at Leslie that way. I'll never have the same talents in all the same areas. But because of her influence, she has inspired me to attempt new things and to appreciate my position in life as a mother and wife. I have learned from her. And even though we live over a thousand miles apart, she encourages me and has made me better in little ways, and for that I'm grateful. Ironically she has said she feels the same way about me. I thank God for her impact and influence on my life, and wish we lived closer so that I could learn even more.

I am reminded that we're all here to learn from each other.

Difficult Distinctions

Years ago when my son was very small, I met a former coworker for lunch. She arrived, still talking on her cell phone. Clearly, she had made a real effort to squeeze in some time to meet for lunch. It was a gesture of kindness. I arrived several minutes before to scope out the restaurant and get Kasey settled. I had packed books, small toys, Cheerios, crackers, and assorted snacks to keep him occupied.

Five minutes after Susie arrived, the crackers and cereal were gone, much of it on the floor after being dropped or smashed. The toys I brought weren't nearly as interesting as the salt and pepper shakers, or the little race car another child had a few tables over. My son was fidgeting, impatient, and could undoubtedly sense my elevated stress level. I was trying to look like I had it all together.

Susie was still in the work mode, but politely inquired how everything was going. While I scrambled to come up with a concise yet honest answer, Kasey spilled his juice at the very moment her cell phone rang.

For weeks, I had desperately needed adult conversation in an adult environment and had been longing for someone to *really* ask me how I was doing, and now I couldn't get an answer out. After an hour of interrupted conversation that barely scraped the surface, Susie had to go, and I was left at the table of a child-unfriendly bistro scooping raisins from the floor and wondering what happened.

I bet many moms have had an episode like this. And though I would never suggest that cutting ties with your working girlfriends is necessary, or even recommended, I am suggesting that stepping away from the workplace will likely change the dynamic of previous work relationships, particularly if your coworkers don't have kids themselves.

Over time, I learned to seek out new friends in my church and neighborhood who were in the same life-stage as me. I needed to invest in new friendships and seek out support groups geared for stay-at-home parents.

Investing in new relationships is not something I used to do all that easily. I'm actually quite introverted, although not shy so much as quiet and hesitant to start up a conversation. So, you can appreciate that it took real effort initially to force myself out of my shell. Sometimes I felt like the only person on the playground that was looking for a friend.

Life Lesson #9. How to be a good friend.

We all know that to have a friend, you must first be a friend. But to be a friend you must see friendship exhibited. It is important whom we call friend, and there are precious few that are truly standing by us when the chips are down. Throughout life, we collect acquaintances and befriend people, but true friendship is a dance of give and take, sensitivity and vulnerability. It requires trust and honesty and allowing ourselves to be real with others. Mostly it takes selflessness. The people who call you friend would be quick to confirm, I bet, that you would drop everything if they needed you. That's the way friendship works. It ultimately puts others before ourselves. That's why we can't be close friends with everyone. Friendship is an investment; it takes time, effort, and energy.

Our friends also reflect the type of people we are—what we value and how we live. My friends are not exactly like me, but we share common components and characteristics. Our appreciation for our differences and our common understandings are part of what binds us together.

Our kids learn the idea of friendship from us. They watch whom we hang out with, observe how we interact with them, and then model it for themselves. My son will have to pick his own friends. I can't do it for him. But I can help him be a better friend to the people he chooses to include in his life and be wise in choosing whom he invests his time with.

Life Lesson #10. Don't be afraid to be your own person. Leaders often stand alone.

Recently a mother shared with me her concern that her son was hanging with the wrong crowd at school. She said he was even aware of the impact of the bad influences and wished to find other friends but was struggling with figuring out how to do that. She wanted to help her son find his own wings so that he could stand and be his own person and not be swayed by the crowd surrounding him. This is an extremely important lesson to learn.

The people we spend our time with influence our speech, our decisions, and our actions more than we might think. It takes maturity to be comfortable in your own skin and be able to influence the crowd you're in, and not have the crowd you are in change you.

If my son is secure in who he is and is motivated by doing what's right versus doing what's popular, he will be able to confidently walk through life as a leader, not a follower.

I can nurture his self-esteem, focus his attention on leaders worthy of following, and help him see what things in life are worth standing firm for. We, as his parents, can support him when he stands alone and encourage him to do what's right even when it's hard.

I cannot, however, make him a leader. I can only help create the environment that breeds that kind of thinking. I can exemplify through my own words and actions that which I try to teach him. And I can surround him with others who are leading and pointing out the trials and temptations of leadership, as well as the joys in the journey.

Giving our son the opportunity to study those who lead in different lifestyles and vocations is important. He sees leadership in action in trusted friends who are doctors, businessmen, missionaries, teachers, and parents. He can learn to serve, to stand boldly for what's right, and to seek to live with integrity and truth, rejoicing in who he uniquely is by God's design.

Chapter 6
New Thinking

*"Teamwork is the quintessential contradiction of a
society grounded in individual achievement."*
~ Marvin Weisbord

*Life Lesson #11. Being independent is good; being
interdependent is better.*

In a culture where independence is not only valued but highly prized, the idea of doing things on our own can be quite appealing. A full 77% of us drive alone, proving that most of us really like being able to go where we want when we want (U.S. Census, 2007). We shop alone, eat alone, exercise alone, and work alone. And according to author Robert Putnam, we are even bowling alone (Robert Putnam, *Bowling Alone* [New York: Simon and Schuster, 2000])! The trends are taking us away from socialization and partnering, and toward isolation and individualism.

While traits of individualism and independence are good, there can be a negative side. Such a lone wolf mentality can lead us to believe that all aspects of life are best conquered alone.

I love tennis. It's a sport I've played since I was twelve. I play both singles and doubles, and they are very different games. One challenging part about doubles tennis is recognizing and anticipating what your partner is trying to do and is able to execute. Every partner will play differently and has their own strengths and weaknesses. For example, if I expect my partner to come forward to the net a lot, when that's not a natural part of their game, I will likely be frustrated when they keep staying back by the baseline. If I expect my partner to keep running down lobs (running back for a ball that has been hit over the head of the net person), and she doesn't move well in those situations, we will be flustered by teams who consistently lob us and will quickly recognize that we aren't working well as a team.

In doubles tennis, the team mentality involves acknowledging that you are working together, connected in heart, will, and purpose. You win together and you lose together. This is a fairly easy concept for team sports players to grasp. Yet I believe most people don't recognize the power of the team mentality when it comes to the family.

Team "Mom"

Over the years, I've met many lonely and overworked mothers. They are unquestionably committed to caring for their families, but an unequal burden of responsibility has left them feeling isolated, unappreciated, and misunderstood. They are home all day without the support they need and feel their husbands are not doing their part or helping to the degree they expected.

"I'm the one up in the middle of the night, every night, when the baby cries, because he needs his rest so he can go to work," one mother shared.

"He doesn't 'get it.' I don't feel like I have any control of my day anymore. I'm just trying to survive. I know I'm not working on some big presentation, but it doesn't make what I'm doing any less important," one mother of twins told me.

These are all very honest statements. It's important to realize that a crucial part of our success in full-time, career parenting involves helping our spouse understand what we're going through and how we need them to actively participate. We have to tell them what we want and need, using clear and reasonable words, and not expect them to read our minds.

Fathers need to be part of the overall vision and understand how important their role is in the parenting process. Sometimes husbands feel inadequate in handling things around the house because of the way we, as women, respond to the help they do give us. Criticism of their efforts certainly doesn't encourage future help.

It's usually believed that when children are preschool age and younger, the role of mother is center stage. There is certainly a mother-infant bond that begins before the child is even born. And though that maternal bond never fully goes away, it is modified and adapted as the father shares a larger role in the parenting journey. At each stage, it is important to consider how both parents can contribute to the ever-changing needs of their little ones in a collaborative way.

A team concept also denotes equality, fairness, and a shared vision. Men generally understand this concept. They tend to spend time very early on working and playing in groups, seeking teams, and competing. They understand the idea of a team. On the other hand, I believe women take on work more individually. We socialize in groups but tend to work alone. Therefore, the challenge is to avoid becoming overly controlling or feeling like a martyr.

It's easy to forget or fail to share our greater vision with others.

Maybe it's because we don't have a clearly defined one, or because we don't see others' roles in it. Perhaps we just aren't good at communicating our need for help.

When we take on too much and see others as not bearing their weight of responsibility, we can become bitter or angry, and we can vent that in any number of ways. For example, we may not share what is really going on with our spouse; we just give them a cold look or harsh words, or suffer silently. I know I've given my husband the silent treatment more than once in our marriage, and it's never solved a thing.

I'm truly convinced that most men delight in their role as fathers and husbands, and deeply love and care for their children and wives. However, the busyness of everyday life and the energy associated with going to work at their own jobs keep many men from having the time to think about the plan they have for their children in any concrete way. They are likely so busy reacting to the work goals in front of them and providing for their families that the concept of strategically planning family goals is not something they have thought of. Men, just like women, have a natural desire to be successful in what they do. They want to have a significant impact on the lives of their family. They want our approval and acceptance. They also crave a vision and a goal to pursue, especially when it comes to the family, and that's where we can help.

Dads today are more open than ever to the idea
of being home with the kids.

"Those who study fatherhood say today's dads are forging a new identity, as working women press for a more egalitarian home life, and telecommuting and workplace flexibility make it possible for dads to have more time with the kids" (Sharon Jayson, "Today's Guys Parent with a New Daditude," *USA Today*, June 17, 2009). There are multiple resources available for men looking to make that transition as well (www.dadlabs.com).

"It's cool to be an active, involved father," says Aaron Rochlen, associate professor at the University of Texas-Austin. "Overall, men being more active fathers is starting to become more of the norm and less of the anomaly."

So, perhaps for your family the right decision involves a different scenario than what used to be considered traditional. One thing can be said about families today—there really is no "traditional."

The Importance of a Shared Vision

Once a year my husband and I spend time evaluating where we are as a couple. We look at our financial goals (both long term and short term), the goals and vision we have for our son, our spiritual growth goals, and our individual goals. We sit down separately and write them out, and then set up a time to get together and discuss them.

Every year we've done this we find we have more and more visions that are shared. It becomes less about us individually and more about us as a family. We are able to feel like a united front on these visions and be a source of support to each other when we have individual goals we want to pursue. It excites, renews, and refocuses us. I am poised to help him achieve all that he wants to be and do, and he knows how to concretely help me pursue my dreams. Our relationship with God, our marriage, and our family are our top priorities.

We work as a team, using our individual strengths to offset one another's weaknesses.

We also have a mutual respect for each other. This is key. It's the only way it will work for us and for any couple. I have to trust him in his role as husband, father, and co-leader, and he has to trust me in my role as wife, mother, and co-leader of our home. And such trust is established over time, reinforced by years of living out a life of integrity and consistency. With trust comes understanding that there is an ebb and flow to life's demands. There are times that we see less of my husband due to travel and commitments at work, and there are times that he is able to work less and give us more of his time. I know in my heart that he wants nothing more than to be home with us, so if he isn't, he's doing his best. I do my utmost to assist him in his efforts so that he can focus on the work he's been called to do. Keeping the distractions and drama away will help him be more efficient with his time, and subsequently be with us more.

Evaluating our goals also forces me to look objectively at the whole package God gave me in my husband. I am better able to understand how he reacts to things and communicates things, and to be able to see him for all that he is.

It's easy for us to want to change our spouse's behavior or be frustrated by what we might perceive as a lack of communication or understanding. But when we see them for who they are (both good and bad) and see ourselves for who we are (both good and bad), we are able to deepen the relationship.

Effectively targeting our goals toward a common front can only be done together, as a team. Otherwise you're pulling in opposite directions and little gets done.

Moms and dads are designed by God to operate as a team. The sooner we unify our visions, the less time we waste and the less frustration we will feel. Being part of a team also helps you avoid feeling lonely, isolated, and unappreciated because you have a partner, friend, and helper to walk the journey with you.

Deepening the relationship with your spouse only deepens your family's bond. It is time well spent and makes your experience as a parent at home so much more rewarding.

It is said that the greatest thing a woman can do for her kids is love and respect their father. Through your relationship with each other, your children first learn the complex language of commitment, love, and unconditional support. How you relate to the co-leader of the family and how you respect his authority set a foundation for what your children understand a home to be.

Little eyes are watching and tender ears are listening. We should make every attempt to provide the environment that ensures what they take in—audibly, visually, and emotionally—is nothing but loving and supportive.

Life Lesson #12. Guard your heart and mind.

It's dangerous to minimize the effect of what's around us. Advertising messages tempt us, video images shock us, music lyrics dull us, media images entice us. We are inundated from the moment we are put into this world until the moment we step out of it. Unless we're living in a remote village in a third-world country, we are surrounded by millions and millions of images designed to motivate us toward believing something, buying something, or doing something.

Your kids are out there in the midst of these images too, only with fewer filters and younger and more impressionable minds.

If we are careless about the lyrics our kids are listening to or images our kids are watching, we set them up for trouble. If we fill their hearts and minds with beauty and truth, they are more apt to see the world that way. If we allow young minds to be filled with jarring images, sexuality, violence, and darkness, that will be the grid by which they see the world as well.

I remain saddened and shocked that so many parents blissfully send or take young children to PG-13 and R-rated movies, expose them to inappropriate music or television, allow violent video games in their house, and pay no attention to what their children are reading or viewing on the computer. Maybe it's a naive belief that they will be able to process such images and information in an appropriate way, or that it isn't hurting anything. But be aware that by the time kids are eighteen, they will have seen two hundred thousand violent images and sixteen thousand murders on television alone. And television is only one form of media they are exposed to.

Part of the importance of parenting is placing guidelines carefully into the family fabric. There should be hard and fast rules about certain things, and for good reason. We worry about child abduction, child trafficking, child abuse and neglect, but we fail to notice that the many cultural influences that threaten to violate the family and the sanctity of childhood are more of a concern. Our kids are far more likely to be influenced by a violent image on a video game or television than to be pulled off the sidewalk and abducted. In a single year, fifty thousand kids are abducted, but a million kids take a gun to school.

Family Vision

I suggest you share your family vision with your children and make their goals part of the plan as well. They will find incredible value in knowing that who they are and what they do factor into your overall family vision and idea of success. The vision becomes real to them, as they can watch the family grow and work toward a common goal. They also mature into adults themselves who appreciate the give and take of a healthy family relationship. They learn to understand the varied roles that each parent plays and can appreciate the delicate balance needed to make a family work.

This is so important. As our kids mature, they are formulating ideas about the kind of spouse they will choose and the type of family they will desire for themselves. Whatever our kids experience growing up sticks. It's wired deeply within them. The more we can teach them about how a healthy marriage relationship works, the more they will be apt to emulate it. The more we can teach them about goal setting, particularly for family and life goals, the better their chances are for success.

Chapter 7
A New You

"If it wasn't for dogs, some people would never go for walks."
~ Author unknown

Life Lesson #13. Take care of yourself.

We are a fitness-obsessed culture. Advertisements abound for the latest healthy juicer, blender, or cooker. Everywhere commercials are selling equipment for abdominal toning, cardiovascular fitness, or overall muscle strengthening. Weight loss plans are presented in every format imaginable. And no one can visit their local grocery market without being presented with a multitude of options, healthy and otherwise. Packaging and food marketing has made most of us label readers these days, and information is all around us helping us consider the multiplicity of food, lifestyle, and exercise options available to us. People seem more aware of the connection between mind, body, and nutrition than ever.

Studies continue to show that there is a huge connection between exercise, diet, energy level, mood, health, and self-esteem. Understanding that connection, clearly, is one key step in your success while staying at home. As the primary shopper, cook, and meal planner for your family, you are the one in the lead in this critically important area. We've all learned that simply feeding your family is not enough.

We are responsible for considering how the foods our
family eats connect to and affect their lifestyle and health.

It's easy to understand how eating properly is essential to the well-being of everyone in your care, including yourself. But just as important is how it also establishes and maintains important lifestyle patterns in your home.

We teach our kids how to eat and how to respond to foods. We are the nutritional coach, so to speak, for we model nutritional patterns that often last a lifetime.

Research shows a direct link between the weight of a mother and the weight of the kids in her care. How moms eat largely determines how kids eat. A healthy mom usually equals healthy kids and family.

Nutrition is something I'm still learning about, because there is so much to know about the food-body connection. I don't eat like I used to when I was single, and certainly nothing like I was raised. As a kid raised in the Midwest, I ate beef, fried chicken, and mashed potatoes. It was a diet heavy on starches, fats, and sugars. Salads had heavy doses of dressing, and fruits were disguised under a warm blanket of cobbler or pie crust. Hot dogs wrapped in bacon were a family favorite, and fish was only fried—I never had it served any other way until I was in my twenties. There was room for improvement.

Certainly, there was nothing horribly wrong with being raised that way. My parents were only feeding me like they had been raised—actually better. As children of the Depression, they often recounted stories of the lengths they had to take to make ends meet. But eating that way now, as a mom, no longer makes sense for my family, and I have the option of making different choices.

Today, we are also more likely to be up-to-date on the latest nutrition and health concerns and are surrounded by information about food safety and dangers. We can't get away from it. Food is no longer just a means to survive; it is a part of our quality of life. We are told that we are what we eat. We eat junk food, and we feel sluggish and unhealthy. We eat well, and we are more likely to be active and healthy. It's not a difficult idea to understand, yet it's often a difficult lifestyle pattern to change.

Exercise is a big component, and it need not be one that requires time away from family. The importance of spending time together fits easily into our need to stay active. Family time can, and should, be a time to go do something together. Most communities have recreation centers set up for family hours at the pool or at the gym, and kids of all ages are welcome. Most health clubs have childcare provided at no additional cost.

I took my son to the gym shortly after he was born. When he was small, I ran around the neighborhood with him in the baby jogger. Many evenings we have walked to the park, thrown a Frisbee in the yard, gone to the driving range, hit tennis balls, walked through the woods...whatever we could think of and whatever sounded good at the time. It didn't matter. We were spending time together, and we were staying active.

Staying active is a constant in my life now, and it's been one thing that has really helped center me.

No Supermodels

I think most women struggle with self-image. It doesn't seem to matter whom I talk to—young or old, thin or shapely, tall or short, athletic or not—almost every woman I know has at least a small problem with her body image. My self-image issues stay more balanced when I stay active. As soon as I stop exercising, I feel sluggish, I eat poorly, I feel guilty about not exercising, and I don't sleep as well. As soon as I resume making it a priority, I feel stronger, eat better, sleep better, and appreciate myself more. I've found that a poor self-image can derail just about anything I attempt. It affects the way I react to others, including my family. It affects the way I carry myself.

It affects my mood, sex drive, concentration, perception of the world around me...everything.

Striving to be healthy has been a progression for me. When I was working and in my twenties, exercise was not really a part of my life. I'd always liked playing tennis, and for many years of my life had played quite a bit, but I had stopped. Aerobics classes were joined and then missed. I walked after work for a while...but only for a while. In general, I chose meeting friends after work or just going home and relaxing over going to the gym or doing something active. I always caught the office "bug." I fought low energy and didn't sleep well. I drank way too much coffee and soda.

Then I met Ken, who worked out a lot and ate really well. He was an inspiration and did all the triathlon sports (swimming, biking, and running). I had become a bit of a couch potato, but I really wanted to share this aspect of his life with him. But, I didn't swim or own a bike, so one day I decided to try running, and over time, I found that I could do something both he and I enjoyed.

I suppose I was lucky to have found something that I could step in and begin doing so easily. Now, years later, I've completed two marathons and countless road races. It spurred an interest in many other physical activities. I got back to playing tennis, the sport I had always loved. I took swimming lessons at forty-three and sailing lessons at forty-five, and I remain convinced that it's never too late to learn something new. It's good to mix things up to keep your exercise routine fresh. Some days I swim, some days I bike, and occasionally I golf or participate in a fitness class. Sometimes I just walk around the neighborhood. The point is that I try to do something nearly everyday.

There is something out there that you can love doing too, even if it's just walking the neighborhood with a friend in the morning or climbing the stairs at the high school stadium. Our bodies are meant to be in motion. It's no surprise that we struggle as a society with weight and weight-related health issues; we don't make exercise a priority.

The late George Sheehan, noted author and runner, used to write about life as a slower, back-of-the-pack runner. He ran much of his life, even into his later years. And though he was never a fast runner, he realized the importance of fitness and fun, and encouraged many, like myself, to just get out there and try. Sheehan wrote, "All of us are athletes. Some of us are in training."

So, I strongly encourage you to seek out that thing that you enjoy and pursue it—for your own health and for the health of your family.

I encourage you to seek out new things to try nutritionally as well. The way I eat now in no way resembles what it used to. My eating and cooking had to change drastically. I was now responsible for the diet and health of others, and my old ways had to go.

But now, armed with a better nutrition plan and more disciplined exercise regimen, I'm stronger and happier with my body image, and it impacts everything I do. And once in a while I can give in to some french fries or a piece of pie and not have to feel overly guilty about it.

I also continue to be reminded that I am modeling how my son views food. If I show him that eating is for comfort, a distraction, or for entertainment, then he will have a different relationship with food than I think is healthy

In my forties now, I'm still not the perfect model of dietary discipline. I skip meals when I know I shouldn't. I tend to overeat the things I love. I still prefer potato chips to raw veggies and hummus, and I get really tired of eating so many turkey sandwiches and carrot sticks. But because I am so acutely aware of the connection between food and my mind, body, health, and mood, I know that food affects me. So, I limit my caffeine, not because that afternoon latte doesn't sound great, but because I know from experience that I get jittery and anxious when I've had too much. I don't eat all the sweets I crave, not because I don't want to, but because it simply doesn't give me the energy I truly need. The reality is I've had to stop following all my natural food inclinations because, frankly, they are not best for me or my family.

Table for One?

I don't know about you, but I hate eating alone. It sounds silly to say it, but when you spend years eating lunch with people, it seems strange not to. During my years in the office, there was always someone to grab a bite to eat with. During the years prior to my son going to school, he was my lunch date each day. But once he went to school, I found I really missed having the company. I missed spending that midday break with someone. Lunches have now become a less important part of my day. I drink a smoothie or eat a sandwich and read the paper or a book, and then get on with my day. Eating at home helps me control portions and make wiser food choices. It's also a great money-saving technique, since eating lunches out can get expensive.

A Break in the Action

Being at home full time doesn't mean you never get a break from the kids. There has to be deliberate time carved out for you. Small breaks during the week help keep your motivation high and your life in balance.

Many churches offer programs like "Moms Day Out," Mothers of Preschoolers (MOPS), and Bible studies that provide childcare. Larger health clubs also offer childcare, and there are day camps available through city zoos, libraries, and community centers that are affordable for most families. Perhaps a neighbor would be open to a cooperative arrangement where you watch her kids for a couple of hours one day, and she returns the favor on another. Maybe a teenage neighbor girl or retiree would like the opportunity to earn some extra money each week. Perhaps you're blessed to have a relative agree to a visit while you get a little time to yourself.

In addition to time away, I urge you to structure within each day, if possible, some personal quiet time, even though this can be hard to find on many days. If your children are infants, nap time is a good time to try. If your kids are older, it's important they learn and observe quiet time as well. Teach them to cherish opportunities to read, listen to books on CD, draw and color, or play quietly. My son used to love spending time in the basement quietly playing with his wooden train set. Children have to know how to entertain themselves for more than just a few minutes. I'm convinced that all kids can entertain themselves enjoyably without the use of a computer, video game system, or television.

It's important to use that time to re-center ourselves. We should be able to take a few moments and breathe deeply, to sense ourselves slowing down and re-centering. Try to pause for a few minutes a day and see how it helps your focus, patience, and mood.

Here are ten things you can try in order to re-center yourself throughout the day:

Ten Cups of Calm, Please

1. Read
2. Call a friend
3. Pray/talk to God
4. Journal
5. Plan your next day
6. Have a cup of tea
7. Close your eyes and think of something beautiful
8. Take a walk
9. Go outside and breathe deeply
10. Work on a project or hobby you love

When my son was small, I needed to recharge around four o'clock each day because it was when I needed it most and was able to find the time. It allowed me time to regroup before I started dinner, before my husband got home, and before my son started to get irritable and need additional amounts of my patience and time. I was able to recharge before I started what felt like the second part of my day.

I wanted and needed to be fresher and calmer, and have things in order for that second half to start. The evening hours sometimes took as much of my energy as the first half of the day did, but I found that how I approached my family at the end of a day was key. If I had things arranged so that dinner could happen at a reasonable hour, we could have time together at the dinner table. When my son was little, Ken played with Kasey while I did the dishes. I joined them afterward and we made every attempt to get our son to bed by eight o'clock.

Even now, after our son is in bed, I try to spend a few minutes focusing on how I can help my husband for the next day. It might include packing a lunch, checking to make sure he's got what he needs for the following day, or just reminding him of upcoming events. I try to remember our team mentality and work together toward our bigger goals. My husband and I are a team. What helps him helps me, and vice versa. When I account for the time he spends driving in the car to and from work, hours spent at work, and the time getting ready for work, I concluded this makes up a lot of his day. I did the math. If I could help him find twenty more minutes in his day, it was huge! He gets little chance to catch his breath before he walks in the door at night. My husband *loves* being the husband and daddy, but it's a big responsibility in addition to being the only one bringing home a paycheck. If I can help him succeed in his many roles, we all win.

Evening time can be couple time—time to talk, share, relax, plan, and enjoy each other's company. I try to resist the urge to put in that last load of laundry or get on the computer to check that last email. I try to make it the time we use to unplug and recharge.

Your husband's commitment to protecting evening time is crucial. You should share in your desire to make it a priority. And while working late from time to time is understandable and usually unavoidable, make sure it's not because home is not a peaceful place to come home to. If your spouse works a late shift and is gone in the evenings or a career involves extensive travel, your family will need to recognize and adjust to the schedule while working creatively together. Often a spouse feels the need to pick up extra hours or an additional job that allows you to stay home. A situation like that is difficult for everyone and a crucial time to stay focused on your goals as a couple and as a family. With the extra pressure he's under and the extra load you are carrying, make sure it is something you both agree to and can handle.

This may sound like a boring life to some, but I've found it's the bedrock of the warm, loving, and cooperative home that many stressed, pressured, exhausted, and hardworking spouses seek. It might be considered old-fashioned, but it will make a difference in the lives of those you love most. Remember it's a team effort, and the goal is a calm, loving, nurturing home. With important work to be done, being there for each other is part of the equation.

It has been said that life is a marathon, not a sprint. The ability to persevere and see the goal out in front is key to our success at home. If we look at the road ahead and not the pebbles in our path, we can keep long-term goals front and center, and we won't get mired in the short-term frustrations or the daily routine.

If we make a plan and have the patience and focus to follow through on it, we can accomplish great things together.

I know that at this time in my life, as a mother and woman who is home full time, I am in a different phase. I won't always be here. My son won't always be young and I won't always be where and how I am today. But I am here now, and I want to adopt, embrace, and cherish what a loving influence I can be to my family as much as I am able. During these career-building and child-rearing years, I want us to succeed as a team. I want us to realize our goals together, collectively, as a family.

There's no better time to focus on your family than right now.

We must not and cannot take a single day for granted. We have an opportunity to realize a healthier and happier life by focusing on our families as the goal, instead of solely our careers. I feel that I am more energized, more connected, and more in touch with God's will for my life than ever before. I also believe that God desires for all of us to be healthy—physically, spiritually, and emotionally—as He is a God of balance. Who we are and what we are work together in harmony—the mind, the soul, and the body. When we achieve balance, discipline, and focus, I feel we can begin to see everything come together.

Chapter 8
A New Future

*"In every conceivable manner, the family is [the] link
to our past, bridge to our future."*
~ Alex Haley

Little girls love diaries. They write in them and cherish them because it is where they can safely share all the thoughts, dreams, and longings of a tender, introspective soul.

Somewhere along the line, I think, women lose that kind of willingness to reveal themselves. We tend to keep our thoughts and dreams private, known only to ourselves, fearing that kind of vulnerability. But when we allow ourselves to be free to reflect and dream, I think we learn who we are and what we really want.

Reading anything I've written ten years ago, ten months ago, or even ten minutes ago reveals much about where I am and how far I've come.

*Keeping a journal during your parenting experience
can be a valuable thing to do.*

I started one when I was pregnant and addressed it to my unborn son. It included the thoughts and fears of a woman staring at motherhood for the first time. As I continued to write throughout his early childhood and school years, the tender stories, funny moments, and random thoughts became a glimpse of who he was and what we experienced. It is a little piece of our history as a family; a written account of how precious, important, and occasionally challenging he was, and how life in general has been. It is a window into my heart, a perspective that is uniquely his to see through. If and when he ever reads it, he will learn something about himself, his father, and me. He will learn about the times in which he was raised and the priority he always was to us.

I believe journaling is a great way to express the moments, difficulties, triumphs, decisions, and uncertainties you encounter. It can also be used as prayer—a private conversation with God. We can express the challenges we face, as well take moments to appreciate the blessings in our lives. Sharing it is up to you. It can be as personal or public as you want it to be. It can simply be a place where you can honestly and safely go and be completely yourself.

I haven't kept a journal every day of my last thirteen years with my son. There have been seasons of introspection and seasons of silence. But what I do have are collections of different thoughts, longings, and musings of a woman navigating her way through motherhood. Each journal, in varying degrees of completion, is saved and put away. The biggest benefit, I think, is that they exist at all. The gift for me is seeing myself within the pages in a way no picture can ever capture. Occasionally I choose to revisit them to give me an appreciation of how far in life I've come.

When I read them, I'm always struck by my honesty. I marvel at how God worked in my life at different times for different reasons. I smile at the things that once frustrated or delayed me and see how I've grown through them and learned from them. I often want to talk to the girl in those pages, to show her how I not only survived but prospered. I want to tell her that the times that were challenging were the times she changed and grew. All these years later, I want to tell her that she will like the person she's becoming.

A friend once remarked that, with the demands of home and family, it was too much to expect to find time to journal. I understand that thinking. I also understand that not everyone is given to enjoy writing as I do. Perhaps a better fit for some would be a scrapbook, or a picture album, or a short listing of "things to be happy about today."

Several years ago, Oprah Winfrey encouraged "gratitude journaling." I've always thought this was a great idea. Sometimes we have to be intentional about recognizing the things we have to be grateful for, because a wellspring of gratitude doesn't always come naturally. Being blessed with the opportunity to see our kids grow up is a big blessing for sure, and having the chance to tell our kids how we feel about them is another.

Life Lesson #14. The blessing of a grateful spirit.

I was at an anniversary celebration and someone asked me about my own family and mother. My mother died over twenty years ago, yet it's still hard for me to speak of her. The woman casually asked how old I was when my mother passed, to which I replied that I was twenty-one. She commented that at least I was lucky it happened when I was all grown up.

It struck me as harsh that she would say that, though I know she never meant it to be. It is commonly thought twenty-one is the advent of adulthood, and it certainly brings a host of adult-like responsibility and respect. But no one I've ever asked over the age of thirty has ever told me that twenty-one is truly grown up. Clearly there is still an abundance of life to experience and knowledge to acquire long after the twenty-first birthday has passed.

My mother died the last day of my twenty-first year, the day before my twenty-second birthday. This personal demarcation line in my life has always seemed remarkable. It certainly taught me how important the first twenty-one years were and how they shaped who I am today. The groundwork was done by then; the foundation of my life was created. At twenty-one, I was far from a finished product, and at forty-six

I'm still not there, but much of who and what I am today is because of those first 252 months.

Now, all these years later, I often wish I had more of a window into the soul of my mother. How did she handle being a mother for the fourth time at age forty-three? What did she think when she was diagnosed with cancer for the first time and had a seven-year-old at home? Did she think she would live to see her fiftieth anniversary? Did she think her mother would outlive her? Was she scared? She never showed it. Was she ever lonely? She never acted like it. Was she happy with her life? She never said.

Now that I am a mother myself, I certainly have a new appreciation for my mother's influence.

How I was treated, disciplined, encouraged, and included in her world has formed much of the framework from which I draw many of my own parenting skills.

My mother was a strong, bright, spiritual, compassionate woman who also was impatient, avoided conflict, and was a bit of a loner. I can appreciate her for what she was and was not. In the brief years I was privileged to be in her life, she taught me through all the spoken and unspoken, difficult and courageous things she did. I remember her good humor and her adherence to her faith even as chemotherapy seemed to be draining the life right out of her. I remember her reading to me, playing the piano alongside me, teaching me to cook, watching me dance and play tennis, cheering me on, and loving me.

I don't remember if every meal was perfect, if the house was always spotless, or if she knew how to do things exactly right. What I do remember is that she believed in me and told me so regularly. I remember she put my needs ahead of her own. I remember her telling me I was special because no matter what, to God and to her, I was.

I remember her giving one of my favorite coats to a third-grade classmate of mine who had none. I remember her urging me to invite kids home for lunch when I noticed they carried no lunchbox. I recall helping her deliver meals to the elderly. And I remember she consistently checked in on friends and neighbors to make sure they were doing okay, yet never complained when they stopped calling and visiting her as her advancing cancer became difficult to watch.

Though she sounds somewhat like a saint as I write this, the truth is, she was just a mom in an average town, living in an average house, with average means, rising to the challenges life threw at her. Through love and perseverance, commitment and faith, she and my dad raised four daughters and firmly established in each of us a picture of what a home is all about.

There was a day when I thought she lacked ambition by not pursuing a career. She had worked off and on over the years doing part-time work, but never really set herself upon any single career course. She always said her job was her family, and she didn't need anything more. She felt confident that nothing mattered if your family wasn't happy, secure, and cared for.

Now I wish I could tell her and show her what I've learned, since I must have seemed so ungrateful at times. I just hope she knows somehow that as a grown woman and mother, I so often reflect on what she taught me.

Painful Reflections

I realize that for some of us, the memory of childhood presents pain and frustration. There may be nothing of your parental example or upbringing you want to emulate. That itself becomes your framework. You uniquely know how those experiences shaped you and what they looked and felt like. You know what it's like on the receiving end of an unhappy home life, and it has formed you in ways you're likely still discovering and recovering from.

We have to come to terms with what we have learned, how we remember our past, and how we are going to choose to improve upon it.

From my own mother's example, I learned that children should never be treated like an intrusion. My mother took me nearly everywhere. I was never made to feel I was in her way or keeping her from doing what she wanted or needed to do. Her telling me I was special didn't give me a massive ego or an unrealistic view of myself but an appreciation for my uniqueness and a boldness to be different.

I learned that it's important for your kids to see you fail once in a while and for them to learn how you handle disappointment.

I learned that faith in God must be the central part of your life or nothing else holds together. I learned that a woman can still be beautiful even if her hair is gone and her health is weakened. I learned that we can have grace, humor, and strength through the most difficult circumstances, that it's up to us.

I realize that how I remember my mother is a tricky thing. Our minds often remember things the way we want to remember them, even though it may not be entirely accurate. I try to be fair in my assessment of my time with her, yet it gets more difficult with every passing year. I was in college when she died, and that's a long time ago now. More time has passed since all the years I shared with her. So, she gets a little more beautiful and her biscuits get even more delicious every time I draw upon those memories...and I guess that's okay. I do try to remember her as clearly and accurately as possible. It's true she wasn't famous. She never went to college or traveled the world. She never climbed a mountain peak or ran a company or a marathon. She was supermom to me, though, not because of her credentials but because she was there for me.

She was there at every stage of my development, and at the end of her life, she was still more concerned with whether I was ready for her to leave than if she was.

I still hope to improve upon my experience by blending the best of her with the unique qualities I have to offer, in concert with what Ken has to offer. My son is a lot like me, but he is not me. He doesn't react the exact same way I would, nor would I want him to. Our home situation is quite different than the one I grew up in. I've deliberately chosen to try to improve upon it in my own ways, and I feel my son deserves all the effort that I can give him. I'm convinced that all any of us can do, as parents, is try to improve upon our past in creating our path to the future.

God put me into the distinct family I was raised in for a reason. I was the fourth of four daughters. I was not the oldest or in the middle but the youngest child, and the youngest by quite a bit. I came along late in my parents' life, making me thirteen years younger than my closest sibling. I don't look much like my sisters, nor share much in common with them. That, too, is all for a reason.

I still can't play Scrabble or piano without thinking of my mother. I hate carnations because she did. Every time I smell Chanel #5 or see a woman wearing a scarf to hide her missing hair, I think of her. Each time I venture to make a pie from scratch, I hear her voice in my ear telling me I'm working the crust too much. I could go on and on.

As little girls we often emulate our mothers, since they are usually the primary female model we see. Just as little boys want to be like their dads, little girls want to be like their moms. Early on, it is her high heels we clomp around in, her coat we wear around the house, and her pearls we try on with our make-believe princess dresses. She is the one we look up to. As girls grow up and appreciate their own personality and place in life, the relationship between mother and daughter often morphs and changes.

I am largely the way I am because of my parents, the good and bad experiences, and the choices I have made over these last forty-plus years. Am I a better mother than my mom? No, I don't believe so.

But I haven't forgotten what I've learned and experienced. I'm able to accept who I am, and I'm not afraid to reach for more.

I'm grateful that I had those years with my mom. Did I once resent not having her for more of my life? Sure. Did I wish she were at my college graduations, my wedding, and the birth of my son? Of course. Do I get teary-eyed whenever I see a young mother shopping or having a lunchtime conversation with her own mother? Naturally.

But I am still grateful. Grateful that I had her at all. Grateful that I was able to witness part of her life. Grateful that I look and act a little like her. Grateful that she left me a legacy of love and faith.

I try to be grateful for most things now. Life isn't perfect. All my hopes and dreams will not be realized. But I know that gratitude gives me peace about what it is I do have. It gives me contentment in the everyday and hope for the future.

I've been given far more than I have given. I've received far more than I've deserved. And when life gets discouraging, I just remember that I've been given so much already and that, perhaps, it's time for me to pay it forward.

What matters now is that we take the experiences from our lives that were good and had value and weave them into our experience now.

We can take our past as a part of who we are and know that it is a piece of our individual story—a story that is still unfolding.

We are born into our specific family for a reason—a reason we may not always see or understand. I'm convinced that I was not meant just to look like my mother but to learn something from her, something that was reserved exclusively for me. God wanted me to learn from her and her alone. And God gave my son to me for a specific reason: to teach him things that only I can teach him. My son never met my mother, but he has seen me and by so doing, he has seen a glimpse of who she was. I'm just passing a piece of her on.

In the 2008 Summer Olympics, the U.S. men's track and field relay gold medal performance was thwarted by the mere dropping of a baton. The lead runner had run an impressive leg of his relay but had been careless with the passing of the baton. It was a relay, and his individual performance to that point on the track meant little because he failed to pass the baton effectively. Hopes fell and gasps were audible as the whole world watched the baton fall to the track below. The next runner could not continue his leg of the race until the baton was recovered, and by then, it was too late. The U.S. team went from vying for a gold medal to not medaling at all. All the years of training and all of the anticipation of victory meant nothing because the one key element of the relay had not been executed well.

We can't drop the baton with our kids. We need to run the race the best we can with as much effort as we can manage, and then carefully, albeit too quickly, we pass the baton on to our kids so that they can keep running well themselves. We have to do the best with what we've been given and try hard to pass something of value on to those who come after us.

It is our own children on whom we have the greatest impact.

It is our children we are uniquely qualified to lead. It is our children who are looking to us and reaching out to us, hoping we will effectively pass the baton to them.

Working outside the home does not make anyone a bad parent. I'm not suggesting that. What I am suggesting is that the real legacy we all seek to leave behind has little to do with our time in the work world.

Our career doesn't define who we are, and it definitely doesn't define who we are to our kids.

What is it we want to be remembered for, and what do we wish our children to recall about our lives? What impact do we want to leave? What excuses are we making for not starting now?

Redefining Our Role

The idea of working is now defined in many different ways. Careers today can often be redefined, readjusted, and reconfigured. A successful job doesn't always need to include excessive time away from family. As women who are or have been in a career, we have a lot of flexibility and choice. We have options, creativity, and the opportunity to define success on our terms. If you make the decision to work in a traditional business setting, you and your family must decide together if it is in everyone's best interest and something you can happily live with. But I would contend that there are many who have never considered other options. They've never truly evaluated the idea of living on one income and are afraid to try. They've never given serious thought to alternatives within their own career field that might allow them more time with their families. They've never pursued other options.

And mostly they've never evaluated how important their individual contribution to their children and family truly is.

In the meantime, I fear, many are letting the busyness of life drive them and ultimately stand in the way of what they really want for themselves and their families.

Sometimes all it takes is a baby step: a small, incremental step toward a better vision for you and the ones you love. One decision at a time. One day at a time.

Just one small step in a new direction can take us down an entirely different path.

Chapter 9
A New World around You

"There can be no vulnerability without risk; there can be no community without vulnerability; there can be no peace, and ultimately no life, without community."
~ M. Scott Peck

We are living in difficult times, with the economy affecting many families with the loss of employment or financial security. Women are a bigger presence in the workplace too and carry more of their families' financial load than ever before.

There are now 3.3 million married couples in which the wife is the sole earner.

That's more than triple the number from 1970. And while 76% of us view more women in the workplace as a positive thing, the majority of us (65%) also admit that having no one home for the children is a negative thing.

We are a busy society. Parents are stretched thin and working hard. Yet, the busyness, stress, and long hours are changing the way our society works, on both a small and a large scale.

Life Lesson #15. Find value in our individual contribution to others.

Being overly involved in our careers can often come at the expense of those around us. The danger is becoming blinded to the needs of those within our families, neighborhoods, and communities.

We might be acutely aware of global needs yet frighteningly unaware of needs closest to us—those quietly hidden behind brick and mortar, fences, and hedges.

Even if we are aware of such needs, our ability to respond to them often feels limited. There is only so much of us to go around, only so many hours in a day, and slowly but surely our feeling of being part of a community slips away. The workplace is often the only community we invest in. And while work is a real community comprised of real people and real ways to help and contribute, it shouldn't be the only one we're a part of.

Big D

Our family lived in Dallas, Texas, in the late 1990s. Dallas–Fort Worth is a big metropolitan area of immense, sprawling suburbs and tall, bricked, fenced-in homes, street after street, in long, treeless uniformity. Most of the newer homes have rear-facing garages emptying into paved alleys. There are thousands upon thousands of suburban houses divided neatly by a small lot and a fenced-in backyard.

Dallas is not unlike many sprawling suburban neighborhoods in metropolitan areas all around the country. Many of today's families, in cities from coast to coast, go in and out of their homes without seeing their neighbors, living years next to people they've never met. And in our transient society, neighbors may only stay briefly before moving on or moving away. People don't make an effort to connect, even when they're only living a few feet away from each other, because they don't make the time or even see the need to. We all know that investing in people takes effort, and it's not always easy.

Community Outreach

As keepers of the home, we are also guardians of the neighborhood and community. We are people all knit together and designed to help, reach out, and love one another. We may feel like islands, but we certainly are not.

It is not accidental that you live where you do or that your neighbors are who they are at this very point in time. I truly believe that God placed you in your city, neighborhood, and moment for a reason, to have your path intersect, directly or indirectly, with a particular group of people. I believe our paths mysteriously connect with others we are meant to learn from, reach out to, support, and love.

Think Globally... Act Locally

I love this bumper sticker. If we think of each other as global brothers and sisters, we should start by being a family to those closest to us. How many of us send support around the world to international charities yet don't know the family across the street or the hallway?

This is also an important idea to imprint in our kids. We can teach them, in real and practical ways, that global love and compassion start within their own neighborhood and community.

When we lived in Michigan, our family created our own community service project. My son named it "Pizza Share," since it involved taking pizzas one Saturday a month to a local family shelter. We learned that the shelter often had plenty of donated food, yet it was often the same thing week after week. Pizza was a treat, particularly for the kids, and they really looked forward to it.

We would go and spread out the pizza boxes on the counter, serving the residents as they walked by. We filled their drinks and cleaned the tables—all very small gestures, but since most had grown unaccustomed to being served, they truly appreciated it. Later we would gather around the various tables listening and chatting, asking about their adjustment there or their prospects for work. Sometimes we would simply sit and hear their stories.

The families at this shelter were staying there for only a short time. Most were just trying to have a safe place to live while they stabilized their lives. Sometimes we would see the same people for a few months, but we generally saw new faces each visit. They didn't know who we were. To them, my blue-jeaned husband was just a nice man who brought his family. My son was just a good boy, kind enough to help the little kids with their food and play with them. And I was just a mom, trying to reach out in some small way.

One Saturday close to Christmas, we brought gift certificates for the residents. We had learned that many didn't have the ability to purchase a gift for a loved one. The gift of giving was not something they could enjoy. We wanted them to have the ability to buy their kids or a family member a Christmas gift, even if only something small.

My son had watched, over the previous weeks, two brothers playing with a single hand-held video game system. Their system was an older one and battered from a lot of use. It wasn't much to look at and had only one game, yet the older brother rarely let the younger one hold it, much less play with it. That same evening, my son, touched by what he saw, gave the younger boy his own system.

Before we left, the mother of the two boys took me by the arm and asked that we wait for one more moment. She whispered instructions to the younger that he should run up the stairs and bring something down. But the boy seemed confused. So the mother asked that we come upstairs to her apartment with them and that it would only take a minute.

We followed her up the stairs to the place that, for that Christmas, they were calling home. Immediately we saw a small but heavily tinseled tree, fully lit with only a handful of wrapped gifts beneath. The mother knelt down, picked up one of the gifts, and handed it to my son. The absence of that gift left a vacancy under the tree. It was wrapped in wrinkled paper, with no bow or adornment—a book, obvious by the feel and size. She insisted that he unwrap it while she and the children watched, and he did. My son, then ten years old, was a proficient reader. The book he unwrapped was for someone just learning to read.

He looked at me, not knowing how he should react. He felt that such a gift was not necessary. He had given his gift out of abundance and had no intention of being paid back. He also knew the book was well below his reading level. Yet, he could see that this gesture was an act of generosity and gratitude. He whispered in my ear that he didn't know what to do. We simply hugged her and thanked her, our hearts touched in a very special way.

On the way home that night, we told our son that the greatest gift for that mother was that she was able to give anything at all. We helped him realize that he could only be gracious in receiving it; the beauty was not in the intrinsic value or usefulness of the gift but in the generosity and the heart of the giver.

We should live out service to others in the world around us but begin in our own homes.

Through selfless acts of service to our kids, spouse, family, and others, we find that gentle spirit within our own hearts and all the energy we will need to pursue truly important work. There are many ways service can play out in our families, neighborhoods, communities, and world. But beginning with our own families, and then moving outward to the circles around us, is one step toward achieving genuine personal fulfillment.

Life Lesson #16. Strive for excellence and never stop learning.

Striving to excel doesn't mean perfectionism, because perfectionism is never attainable. We live in an imperfect world and we are imperfect people. Striving to excel means setting the bar high and doing our very best. Less than our best may get the job done. Less than our best may impress others. But less than our best is less than our best, and it should not be a pattern we continually fall into.

Conversely, our best will sometimes mean we lose. It might mean we fail. But I want my son to know that doing his best is something he can be proud of and learn from. And only he will know if he truly did his best. I can't judge that for him. I do know, however, that the things he will look back on as those he's most proud of will be those he gave his best to. He'll also recognize later on that the things that challenged him the most helped him grow the most. Hopefully he'll look to what he can learn from failure and how he can serve others through his success.

As parents, we have been given a job to do. The honor comes in understanding our responsibility, stepping up to it, and giving our best. Putting all our energy into working and striving can threaten to deaden and desensitize us.

It's far too easy to create a life that doesn't allow the sensitive side of us to emerge. Researchers have even labeled our reaction to the overwhelming amount of need presented to us via the media. It's called compassion fatigue, and it is a syndrome pervasive among Americans today. We have stopped reacting in significant ways to the need around us because we have become desensitized to it.

I found that when I stepped away from the work world, I didn't become more compassionate; I simply became more aware and more able to respond. Time away allowed me to reflect, re-prioritize, rejuvenate, and re-introduce myself to the world around me. I saw a whole world I'd been missing.

Part of Starbucks's success stems from their ability to replicate the idea of community in neighborhoods across the United States.

Employees are trained to be personable and even commit individual names and drink orders to memory. Founder Howard Shultz placed espresso machines in his stores in 2008 with a low-profile design so that employees behind the counter could be seen and interacted with. The very idea for Starbucks originally came from European cafes where people gather and meet. If customers are recognized and appreciated in a personal way and made to feel they are a part of a community, they will make visiting and patronizing it part of their lifestyle.

It certainly worked for me...and I'm not the only one.

Serving Others

—ᴡᴡᴏᴏᴄᴇᴛᴏᴏᴛᴏᴏᴏᴡᴡ—

Just remembering that we are part of a larger community—bound together by how we live, seek balance for our families, earn a living, and want to love and be loved—makes us all feel a part of one another.

—ᴡᴡᴏᴏᴄᴇᴛᴏᴏᴛᴏᴏᴏᴡᴡ—

Expressions of kindness exhibited within the community don't have to be elaborate. Simple gestures can include interacting with the person working the register in the grocery store or learning the name of the person making drinks at your favorite coffee stand. It could be a wave or a simple thank you, a smile, or a card. It could be remembering that even telemarketers are people too. Get creative and be bold, and then watch how people respond.

One winter day in Ohio, I brought a cup of hot cocoa to the man working at the car wash because it was thirty degrees and windy outside. He was totally blown away (literally and figuratively). It was such a simple gesture toward him, yet such a huge blessing for me.

Random acts of kindness are also fun. The smallest efforts seem big in what at times can be a thankless and unappreciative world. In them, you'll see how important your individual role in life is, how the small things you do can make such a big impact.

Sometimes we make a small impact, sometimes a large one, but we are definitely more apt to influence and impact others in the pool of life.

One of the best things I discovered after stepping away from my career was reconnecting with the part of myself who cared about and made time for others. I volunteered from time to time during the years I had worked but generally didn't make time for any significant contribution. Since my son frequently sees me serving others, he has learned the importance of kindness to others.

Teaching our children that we respect and honor service gives them a platform to seek ways to serve others themselves.

It makes a lasting impression and is the foundation of teaching the next generation real ways of living out a life of compassion and kindness.

A friend once told me that rather than calling them "random acts of kindness" we should instead speak of "intentional acts of goodness." She's right. Random acts are great, but intentional acts are even better. Let's be intentional about our efforts to help each other, seeking to use our time away from the workplace wisely.

Skimming Rocks

I love the serene and calming nature of water. My son likes it too but would rather jump in it, swim in it, and throw rocks into it. As a little boy he liked to go to our neighborhood lake, toss a pebble, and watch the ripples he created. Then he would toss a larger rock and see the difference. He learned early: small rock, small ripple; large rock, large ripple.

I believe that by making acts of kindness an intentional part of our life, we are like these rocks.

We are able to reach more, do more, and affect more simply because we dared to put ourselves out there and try.

Chapter 10
A New Conviction

*"If you don't love what you do, you won't do it with
much conviction or passion."*
~Mia Hamm

Months into my journey of staying home, I became frustrated and fatigued. It felt like no one was noticing or appreciating what I was doing. I had lost my enthusiasm and energy, and days started to run together with what felt like not much accomplishment. My toddler son was incapable of discussing the finer literary points of *Guess How Much I Love You*. My hair was always in a ponytail. I felt frumpy and tired, and the housework felt overwhelming. I gave serious consideration to going back to work, leaving the childcare and home matters to others more qualified.

One night, I talked to my husband about how hard this was for me. I probably didn't even let him get a word in. I needed to vent about the long days, constant responsibility for another human being, tedious diaper duty, boring and unending housework, and my loss of identity. I needed to have him reaffirm just how important this decision was to all of us.

*I wanted to hear that besides still being a productive member of society, I
was also still attractive, interesting, and, most of all, normal.*

It was easier for him, he admitted, to have confidence that things at home were being handled while he was gone each day. It gave him the freedom to concentrate on matters at work and was a blessing for him to know he could trust me with the care of our son and management of our home. He hugged me and assured me that I was, in fact, quite attractive, interesting, and, yes, even normal.

I've heard from many parents that the feelings I expressed during this life-stage were not unusual. It's common to feel out of sorts with the new role parenting brings, particularly the new role stay-at-home parenting brings. Early parenthood can be a stressful time for couples, as the needs of the children threaten to overrun everything else. It's hard for most families to find a necessary balance. For those who have been staying home raising and caring for the children, it's often a time when frustration and fatigue are greatest and the temptation to go back to work is strongest.

For most new parents, months after the euphoria of having a newborn is over, life settles into a routine and what seems like an ever-changing set of challenges. In many families, there are multiple kids to consider, with multiple schedules to respond to. It's busy, crazy, and tiring, but it's also a time of precious memories and unexpected joys. The early childhood years should be a time to focus on the goals you set as a couple, but they do require a great deal of flexibility.

Remember that important groundwork
is being laid during these early years, and patterns are
being established. It's investment time.

Prior to making the decision to stay home with your children, your family will, undoubtedly, consider the practical things that need to happen. But most couples fail to discuss the emotional and social changes this new family decision will bring. Finding emotional support, exhibiting loving communication and gratitude, and dealing with changing identities are matters that are often not explored. Not surprisingly, when frustration or conflict appears, it can often be traced back to one of these core relational issues.

Lack of communication and changing priorities are numbers three and four of the top ten reasons couples divorce.

Clearly families can be damaged if these things are left untreated and unresolved.

It is important to discuss with your spouse and family just what kind of support mechanisms you will need to feel confident, valued, and appreciated. Initially, I didn't know what I needed; I learned over time.

Love Languages

The Five Love Languages by Gary Smalley is a quick and helpful read. It categorizes people in terms of the ways they communicate and receive love. Each person is a blend of types but usually gravitates toward one or two specific preferences. For example, I am someone who likes verbal affirmation and who highly values the time people spend with me. My husband also responds well to verbal affirmation, but, like many men, appreciates physical touch.

There are many personality studies that can help us understand one another. Businesses commonly use them to help employees understand and communicate with one another. It is certainly no less important to understand the personality types living within our own homes. (If you're interested in better understanding your personality and those of your family, the Myers-Briggs Type Indicator is an interesting tool to consider.)

You should discuss family issues with your spouse on a regular basis. Consider asking just a simple question or two specifically relating to your job at home and the goals you're both trying to achieve. Help your spouse understand what kind of feedback you are looking for. It's a great way to revisit the plans you laid out and to make sure you're both on the right track.

Discussion questions might look something like this:

1. What has been your biggest challenge this past week? How can I help?

2. What milestones have you seen with our child/children?

3. What have you learned about yourself lately?

4. What can we do as a team to improve upon what we're doing here?

5. What has been the highlight of the past week?

Persistence

It can be tempting during the course of full-time parenting to lose your focus and motivation. I have often struggled with persisting, particularly when the days get long and I get weary. As a stay-at-home parent, staying on track and maintaining your momentum can be difficult on many levels.

My husband is great at keeping a fixed goal in mind. He encourages me to persist in anything I choose to do, even when I'm tempted to quit or get discouraged. Ken also has a unique perspective of life. He doesn't sweat the small stuff, quickly discerning between what is truly important and what is not. He never confuses the two and helps me look ahead to better things when my tendency is to look down.

Ken has his own story to tell. Years ago, his understanding of faith, persistence, and personal identity was shaken to the core and tested beyond imagination. So, if I dare speak of persistence, especially in the face of adversity, I must include him.

In 1991, Ken was a twenty-nine-year-old marketing executive and triathlete in peak physical form. Early one August morning, he and his friend were riding their road bikes in preparation for an upcoming triathlon. They often biked a patch of sparsely traveled road in Kansas, and chose it partly because of the lack of traffic they saw.

This particular morning, a woman driving in the opposite lane on her way to work fell asleep at the wheel and veered suddenly across the road. The car hit them head on at a combined impact speed of seventy miles per hour. Ken was biking in front, and the collision sent him into the grille of the car, then into the windshield, and eventually under the back wheels, where he was crushed. His riding partner was flipped, landing in the ditch nearby. Both men were gravely injured.

Ken lay in the road with multiple fractures to both of his legs, his pelvis, right shoulder, and right arm. His injuries were severe and there was massive blood loss. Two paramedic units arrived; the incident miraculously happened during a shift change when both were available. Months of surgeries and rehabilitation awaited Ken.

He was taken from the best physical shape of his life
to the lowest point he had ever been.

Yet this is just the beginning of his story.

Ken was told he'd never run again or have a normal life. He was told to prepare himself to be an amputee. His plans would have to be different, as his career would be stalled or possibly over. Nothing was going to be the same again.

But Ken wouldn't accept that. He still wanted a lot out of life, and though circumstances had changed and the timeline had been altered, his dream remained constant. He wanted a full life with a family and a fulfilling career. It was going to take more time and considerably more effort now, but he wasn't abandoning the dream.

Nearly twenty years later, you would never know anything happened to Ken. Many people meet him today and are completely unaware of that fateful event in 1991. He would end up keeping his arms and legs, learning to walk again, and, in the coming years, competeing in triathlons, half marathons, and bike races. He has the scars and enough metal in his body to make airport security interesting, but Ken is as happy and satisfied a man as you will ever meet.

Recovery meant years of rehabilitation and multiple surgeries, uncommon will and determination, but Ken is now living the life, as a husband and father, he always dreamed of.

Though many assumed he must have been forgotten by God that day, Ken will be quick to tell you that he saw the Lord's intervention, grace, and love in a greater degree during his trials than at any other time in his life.

To me, Ken is persistence personified. If it meant awakening each day to excruciating pain and forcing himself to physical therapy, he'd do it. If his physical therapist gave him a goal of walking five laps around the track behind a shopping cart or with a cane, he did ten. Regardless of what people said or the odds stacked against him, Ken stubbornly refused to give up.

He kept his eye on the goal: walking, running, and biking again, and living a full life. This included, he hoped, a wife and family. He never took his eyes off the prize. Doctors told him he was in denial, that it was unrealistic to expect to do what he hoped to. No one, in their experience, had ever come back from something like this.

But Ken was undeterred, unwavering, unrelenting in his pursuit of that goal, and persistence paid off. He resumed a normal life, and his persistence gave him a newfound lease on life.

The persistence I refer to within the parenting experience might seem unrelated to such a dramatic and inspirational story, yet we can all appreciate how difficult life can be when we are met with unexpected challenges. It's not always something dramatic that knocks us down and threatens to take us off track. Even minor things can weaken or overwhelm us. Yet, like Ken, we must keep our perspective in check and keep our eyes set on the goals we envision for ourselves.

Don't Lose the Vision

Regardless of our background, education, or experiences, we each have the opportunity to create a strong, healthy, and loving family life. If that's your goal, it will take effort and time, but I encourage you to persevere. Don't be discouraged by frustrations, fatigue, or failures. Keep your eyes looking forward, and don't give up on yourself or your family.

Recently I watched a nature movie with my son. The beauty of animals in their natural habitat is one of my favorite things to see. The most incredible part of this program was watching a leopard chasing his prey. What amazed me most was that the leopard never took his eyes off the animal he was chasing. Never. The terrain changed, the direction of his target changed, the speed at which he ran changed, but his eyes never stopped focusing on the goal that he was chasing.

It is that same laser focus that allows us to do our best work as parents, and it is unwavering and dogged persistence that gets us through the tough days to move on with the important goals we have set.

Chapter 11
A New Moment

"Today is a gift; that's why it's called the present."
~ Author unknown

W̶e live in a fast-paced and media-soaked culture: viewing, texting, tweeting, and chronicling our lives in meticulous detail on blogs and webpages. We are fascinated by the vast amount of information we can access, the ability to communicate with others worldwide, and the random musings and activities of others. Meanwhile, keeping up with all of it takes up quite a bit of our collective time. The average person, according to Nielsen Research, watches over thirty hours of television a week, and no less than four hours a week is spent on the internet. This, of course, doesn't account for cell phone usage—minutes used each month varies widely depending on our age, although 36% of us express shock each month when we get our bill.

We are distracted and over-stimulated by everything that has become part of our culture, often at the expense of relating to our kids.

We're busy, busy people. And research shows it's stressing everyone out.

"When [a] parent or child is plugged into a BlackBerry, cellphone, video game, or television, they're not going to have enough time for issues like [stress] to come up," says Katherine Nordal, clinical psychologist and executive director for professional practice at the American Psychological Association. According to her 2009 study, 85% of kids surveyed said they weren't comfortable talking with mom or dad because their parents were so busy.

We're either on our way to something or doing something all the time, leaving little time to stop and take a breath. And living in the moment is as much a struggle for me as anyone, so I know how easy it is to get distracted and miss what's really important.

I remember certain things, like watching the sun set on a particularly beautiful night in Ohio, getting caught in a rainstorm in the middle of a run, smelling the freshness of pine and fir in a forest in Colorado, and hearing my son laugh for the very first time. These are simple examples of when everything stood still, if only for a moment, and I was truly drinking in life and appreciating every detail.

Most of the time, on any given day, I'm missing it—missing the moment, brushing by the beautiful normalcy of an average day.

Life Lesson #17. Cherish the moment you're in.

So I wonder, how different would our lives look if we were able to live in the here and now more frequently? How different would our lives and our parenting be if we had, at least part of the time, more recognition of the brevity of life and responded to it in that way? What would happen if we taught our kids that stress doesn't have to be a driving influence in our lives?

We've heard it said that kids grow up fast, but of course, as any parent can attest, you don't realize how fast until it is your kids you are watching change right before your eyes. It's alarming and unsettling to see just how rapidly your child goes from learning to walk and talk to being a person with their own opinions and tendencies. One day they're in diapers, the next day riding a bike, the next driving a car.

When our son, Kasey, was first born, my husband, in moments of joyful new fatherhood, would come home from work each day and proceed to shoot an entire roll of film of our son.

"He's changed so much," Ken would say, to which I would respond, "Since yesterday?"

To him, our son was morphing right before his eyes. It's true that babies in that first year grow and change at an astonishing rate, but I didn't realize how much back then.

Now, looking back at the fourteen years behind us, I desperately want to slow down the clock for the upcoming years. I have no desire to have them go as fast as the last fourteen went. That sober reminder is what keeps me focused on the day I'm in—worrying less about the future and doing what I can today. I must constantly remind myself to use my time wisely and invest in my son now. Chances are, he will remember the unplanned, unstructured, and unexpected moments most…the ones I'm likely to dismiss or pass over as unimportant. I know that each day is an important day, even if I may not see it that way at the moment.

Parenting young children is a unique and wonderful life-stage, a foundational time in our children's lives.

The patterns, priorities, and principles that are established within our homes now are what our kids will take with them into adulthood.

Yet these years, traditionally, are the ones when most careers are in full swing. Juggling work and family is a difficult balance. That's why so many people struggle to get it right. It can be easy to fall prey to the idea that time is best spent on a career now, with ample time to spend with kids and loved ones later on. "Work hard now...enjoy life later."

Within that mind-set is the assumption that health and spiritual and emotional well-being can be controlled and managed. Until something happens, like an unexpected test result from the doctor or the loss of a job, it's easy to forget just how key this moment right now, this particular moment, is in the life of your family.

As we wait for that next opportunity, level, or career goal, we often lose sight of the fact that time that we can't retrieve is going by, and that we are needed by our families, right here and right now, more than ever.

Relationships do not remain healthy and stable if they are not tended to. In fact, just the opposite will happen. All things, especially our families, get weakened over time if not infused with new energy and effort.

My husband is the gardener in our family. I will go along to the nursery and help pick out the plants, and maybe even help put a few in the soil. But when it comes to watering them daily, weeding them, and tending them...I'm out. I've moved on to other interests, which for me means just about anything but that. My husband, on the other hand, takes as much joy in tending the garden as any other aspect of it. He loves watching the little plants grow to bigger plants and seeing trees and flowers react to different stimuli. He'll move plants around to other spots if he determines they aren't flourishing. He reads gardening magazines and jokes that passing four greenhouses on his way home from work every day is pure torture. I have no patience for gardening. Over time, the plants inside our house usually die and are replaced by what I consider lovely silk arrangements. Ken sweetly endures my fake plants inside because of the natural beauty he gets to enjoy outside.

It's foolish to believe that a garden can maintain itself while the gardener completely dedicates himself to something else. Everything will look fine for a while, but over time, the plants will be overrun with weeds, threatening to choke out what was originally intended to grow.

When a child's life is not nurtured with the seeds of love, security, value, and discipline, the weeds of disdain, insecurity, apathy, and lack of respect grow. I believe that children seek out fundamental parameters in their lives to guide and direct them. Children will find what they need within their own families, or they will go looking for it elsewhere. We have to invest in our families with our time and ourselves now.

Nothing else can truly replace the time we spend with our children, and no one else can replace what we are to our families.

When we don't make time for our kids, we inadvertently show them that they have little value to us. If we are able to exhibit to our children that they have great value and that they are loved by God and by us no matter what, they won't need to seek affirmation elsewhere.

If we are consistent in our words, loving in our actions, and selfless with our time, our children will trust us, respect us, and want to be around us.

Insincerity doesn't work with kids. They sniff it out and reject it. They are constantly watching and learning from what they see around them as they begin to formulate their own sets of standards and values. Kids want to know what's real and to be able to see how real people handle real situations within their own homes. The lessons of integrity and character start here, and they start early.

Even preschool children are looking for authenticity to begin building their emotional framework. They learn trust or distrust from the behavior of those around them, and they learn it in a variety of ways. Kids are never too young to understand what is going on, and they are watching more closely than we realize.

It's the investment we make now, in the shared family vision and the time we give to the people and things that truly matter to us, that will make a difference.

Parenting is not something we can or should be able to delegate. Raising our children is not something better left to others.

Listening with My Latte

One morning at my favorite coffee shop, I overheard an interview between a working mom and a prospective nanny. The nanny was a college student attending night school and looking for employment during the day. The mom came well prepared for the interaction. She had three pages of notes detailing what a day would look like caring for the two children in her home. Item by item she went, trying to impress upon the prospective nanny the importance of maintaining a schedule, planning activities so her children wouldn't be idle, appreciating nap schedules and mealtimes, and actively participating in the discipline and education of the children. For nearly half an hour I listened as the college student politely nodded and then slouched impatiently in her chair. I listened as this mother of two attempted to consolidate the day's expectations and experiences into thirty minutes and three pages.

What I wanted say to the mother is that she was missing it. If she could hear herself talking, she would realize that what she considers to be simply the minutiae of life at home with her kids takes talent, perseverance, love, dedication, creativity, and a strong set of values. It's not just a "job," as the potential nanny viewed it. Clearly all of it was important to the mother or there would be no need to go over, in painstaking detail, the dance of caring for children she was trying to replicate.

I wanted to say, "My dear woman and fellow mother, are you listening to yourself? Is there anything more important than the life of your children, the childhood experience of people you love? Are you content to leave this important job to anyone else, particularly someone with the life experience of a twenty-year-old, disinterested and sitting back in her chair?"

Unfortunately, we don't get second chances when it comes to childhood. We get one shot at it, and then we're done.

Poor parenting decisions can leave scars. We don't forget who made time for us and who didn't. If we learn that love is somehow conditional on our performance, we spend the rest of our lives performing or fleeing anything or anyone that requires such conditions. If we see a lack of commitment in our parents' relationship toward one another or toward us, we often hesitate to commit to deep and lasting relationships ourselves. If we learn that love is done only when convenient, when we find out that love is often inconvenient, we are unprepared to handle it.

Life Lesson #18. Love is a commitment.

Kids want and need to come first in their parents' eyes. They are looking for love and support, and to be nurtured and taught. They need stability, faith, and trust, and to find role models in their mom and dad. Children need to know that they are in a unique relationship with their parents that cannot be replaced by a hobby, a job, or any creature comfort. They need to know that the security of that relationship is there so that they can have the wings to venture out and discover the world around them. Children want and need boundaries from their parents to make them feel secure and loved.

That's part of why parenting is such a big deal. We are irreplaceable. No one else has the impact on our kids that we do, so we must invest and be involved.

I sometimes marvel that a single school report can cause so much angst for my son. I've written hundreds of reports and thousands upon thousands of words. I've been in stressful situations before—many, many times—and I've known what it is to worry about something that seemed monumental. But my son hasn't. I sometimes forget, thinking, "It's just a report. Just write it already. Do this and do that, and you'll be done and it will be great." But he looks at it as this incredible challenge and wonders how he will ever find the time to research it and be able to find the words to write it. He needs my help.

*I won't recognize those teaching moments or respond to them
appropriately if I'm not living in the present and making time for
him when dinner is calling, the phone is ringing, and the service man
is on the front porch waiting to be paid.*

I'm convinced that many of the pressures of adolescence would be unappealing if children knew that their parents were standing in their corner, actively making room for them even when other things are tugging on their time and energy. I'm likewise convinced that many of the challenges of youth would be easier to handle if kids felt they were uniquely bound to their parents by love, respect, and trust. When parents are leading, the kids learn leadership. When parents are loving, kids learn how to love.

We know that kids don't need designer clothes, the latest computer game, a closet full of toys, a big house, or to ride in a new car, yet so often we perpetuate that very mind-set. Kids would gladly forfeit the latest gadgets if they could find their value in the eyes of their parents. No one wants to feel they are an inconvenience. It's certainly no fun being around distracted, stressed-out people who are having difficulty deciding what their priorities really are.

Human spirits are so tender, impressionable, and malleable in the early years. God gives children this amazing natural desire to be with their parents.

They actually want to be around us, learn from us, and grow with us. They want to see approval in our face and hear it in our words. They long to see themselves in us, in some small way, so that their world makes sense to them. We have to be careful not to quash that or to take it for granted.

A father once told his grown son, a busy physician and father of three, not to forget that during the early years his children are watching him and looking up to him. "They're under your roof now. You have their eyes and ears now, son. In a little while you'll find yourself chasing after them," he said wisely.

And so it is. A few brief years of influence followed by a lifetime of watching the people you helped create live out their lives. A few brief years of their unfettered adoration, and a lifetime of watching them walk farther and farther away from you as they go down their own life paths. It's a natural process, and it's not an easy one, as any parent of a teenager or grown child can attest.

My son's sixth grade class trip was out of state. I was one of about thirty parents that came alongside to watch and assist. I went not because the trip in and of itself interested me so much but because I felt it would be a good opportunity for me to watch my son in his school habitat and to help if needed.

I expected some distancing as he hung with his middle school buddies. I expected some coolness as he asserted his independence in new ways. I expected some over-stimulation, knowing that his diet and sleep would be greatly altered and would take its toll.

What I didn't expect was to be largely ignored. I wasn't ready for that.

I realize that the mother-child relationship is a precious and ever-changing thing, and that it's hard to go from varying states of dependence to a state of complete (or trying to be complete) independence in what seems like the blink of an eye. And to be fair, he never meant to ignore me. He didn't see it that way. He was twelve. He was just being a preteen, having fun and exploring a new sense of space, which at this time didn't include me. As soon as we returned home, everything was normal again. His behavior on the trip was just one small step in negotiating and exploring where he will be within the delicate balance in the healthy parent-child relationship. My own reaction was a wake-up call that my little boy was growing up. My own sensitivity to it was a lesson that I can and should do all I can to raise and nurture him but that his independence is inevitable and a desirable part of maturing.

It served to remind me once again that the precious time
I have with him will someday be over.

It might be next year, in five years, or in fifteen years, but it will end. My primary influence will be squeezed out by a variety of different people and different things, and I, in small emotional and physical ways, will spend my lifetime chasing.

Chapter 12
A New Decision

"The refusal to choose is a form of choice; disbelief is a form of belief."
~ Frank Barron

A decision is like the first step on a ladder. You're going up, or you're getting down. A decision is a point of commitment where you consciously and deliberately determine a direction for your life.

It is a decision to pick a certain school or college. It was a decision when you did or didn't choose a spouse. It is a decision to choose a career path, have kids, buy a house, or pursue a relationship. All of these decisions eventually become the landscape in our life's topography. Like planting a stake in the ground, decisions become demarcations. From them, we set a course of action, moving off in different directions that are either positive or negative. With them, we build a blueprint for our lives.

Though it may not feel like it, life decisions are always taking us in one direction or the other.

We can never truly stay in a neutral position. If we commit to something, we've moved; if we haven't committed, we've also moved.

When we commit to something, we have shifted into a position of motion toward a specific destination or goal. And similarly, when we fail to commit, we have also moved, often away from things that will teach us, challenge us, and help us grow.

Failing to commit is usually easier. It comes naturally to us and doesn't require effort, determination, or vision. Commitment, on the other hand, is almost always hard. It requires risk, energy, persistence, and faith.

When I was twelve, my grandmother Lora died. She was my last living grandparent and the only one I had ever known. I don't remember much about her, but I remember the day of her funeral very well.

The family was gathered for a viewing, and I was the only child there. It was easy to get lost in the busyness of the day. Curious by nature, I slipped out and wandered the hallways of the building. Through a door with "Chapel" written above it, I quietly and slowly walked into what, I thought, must be a place of reverence. Clearly God was here, I concluded; it was so peaceful and pretty. It was only a small chapel with little adornment or decoration, only a handful of pews and a cross on an altar near the front.

I had grown up going to church and had seen my mother pray and speak often of her faith during the many years she was ill. I had also witnessed the strength she had gained from her faith. I knew my grandmother went to church and could play hymns on her old out-of-tune piano, but I had no idea what her relationship with God was like. Did she pray? Did she trust Him? Did she expect to see Him when she died?

I knew that I did and that I wanted to make sure that God knew I did too. So, as an awkward twelve-year-old girl, I knelt in that little chapel and talked to God as if He were sitting right beside me. I told Him that I wanted to be with Him someday and that while I was here on this earth, I wanted to hear, know, and trust Him. And as I walked out into the bright hallway and from then on, although in growing and changing ways throughout my life, I have learned that God is there for me, as close as a friend.

Skeptics will likely pass this incident off as a little girl, with childish dreams and understandings, creating in her own mind someone and something she could hold onto. But, I know this: there was a presence that day in that chapel—a presence I truly believe was God Himself. He heard my prayer. I left there that day feeling noticeably changed, knowing I was a child of God. I had committed my life to Him.

Over the years I have learned more about who God is and have experienced enough life to know that I can trust Him even when I don't understand His plan or timing. I can trust Him with the small details of my life just as much as with the big ones. I have learned that God always has my best interest at heart, that He loves to make good out of bad, and that His ways are never the ways I envision.

When it came to making the decision to stay home, I talked to God a lot. He would have to lead me, or I knew I would lose my way. I knew even if He was leading me to do something that felt hard, scary, or unknown, I could trust Him for the outcome. I knew that He would enable me, support me, and lead me through any endeavor, particularly this one. And I knew that if God was telling me to do something and it was consistent with what I knew about Him, it must be the right thing to do.

Over these past several years, I have been able to step away from the maddening noise of work matters and career competition. It has enabled me to discover what I feel is my real calling. I believe that the things we're really supposed to be doing in this life aren't always the things that we struggle the most with. As it says in Ephesians 2:10, I believe that God equips each of us "to do good works, which God prepared in advance for us to do."

I believe that God has equipped me to be a mother, the best mother possible for my son. It's not arrogance that makes me say that but confidence. God gave my son to my husband and me, not some celebrity couple or the neighbors next door. He specifically gave him to us because He has things uniquely planned for us to teach him and learn from him. God gave us our son because He knew, in the way only He can, that my son would be best suited to be raised in the environment we're in, the time we're living, and the geographical point we call home.

Even through hardship, kids are meant to experience life, to learn and grow in specific ways God has already planned.

I was not born a child of privilege or poverty. I was somewhere in between—where most of America lives. I was not born in India, China, or the Outback of Australia but right in the middle of the United States, in the state most people drive through or fly over on their way to somewhere else. I was not born on a farm or in the city but in a midsized Midwestern community in a hardworking neighborhood of truckers, factory workers, teachers, and laborers. I speak from the middle of everything. I have known what it is to wait until payday before I could pay bills and go to the grocery store, and I've known what it is like to have financial security and my cupboards stocked. I've known heartbreaking loss and surpassing joy. I've known the pain of childbirth and, through it, the gift of motherhood. I have known what it is to love and be loved. I am just like you...not in every way, but in many ways. I speak to you as one who has lived within God's will for my life and as one who has not.

That twelve-year-old girl grew up and encountered trials, temptations, and times of wandering and failure. I once thought that life was best figured out on my own. I claimed to know God, yet I put Him on a shelf because He felt at times distant and disinterested. I didn't have a fully formed idea of God and didn't really know what I believed in, so I couldn't verbalize my faith when confronted or truly rely on my faith when challenged. I stumbled through my twenties learning that my life wasn't at all what I thought it was about. It wasn't about me and my plan for my life; it was about God and His plan for my life.

This understanding changed everything.

This new vista provided the perspective I needed. At age twenty-eight, on a gray winter day while sitting in my car in the middle of a city park, I tearfully, but completely, committed to turning over my life, and how I lived it, to God, trusting Him to have a better plan for me than I did. It was only then that life got really interesting, fun, and meaningful. I can't imagine living life any other way, and so I urge you to pause and consider where you are, right now, with God.

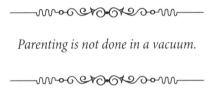

Parenting is not done in a vacuum.

We don't do any part of life on our own, because we can't. We don't control anything about our lives; we only think we do. I can't say I'll be here tomorrow because I simply don't know. All I do know is that I am dependent on something greater than me, not only to keep my heart beating and my lungs breathing in and out but to orchestrate the entire symphony that is my life. That something is someone, and that someone is God.

There are nearly seven billion people living on this planet,
each with their own desires, dreams, and destinations.

Now imagine each of these seven billion people being created to do something unique and special, something that God intended for them to do. Imagine that to be true for you. Imagine the God of this universe specifically giving you a gift set of talent, treasure, and time. Consider that He wants to help you achieve the use of those gifts to the fullest extent possible, that He wants you to know joy, peace, and fulfillment in your life, and that most of all, He wants a relationship with you. Imagine what your life would look like if you knew that this were true. It would be amazing.

I cannot parent effectively without realizing the leadership and love of God. And I sincerely believe that no one can ultimately reach his or her potential without trusting and knowing God, and letting Him direct your path and light your way.

Many people who are considered successful in this world don't know where they are with God. From the outside they can, and often do, appear to have it all, but internally I am convinced they are missing the lasting significance and meaning that only a life with God can offer. I live in this world and so, like you, am challenged to not measure myself by the world's standards. I have to remind myself that the world's standards are not the ones I need to be striving to achieve. As Philip Yancey puts it, I must play to an audience of one. My desire is to please God and to live the life God designed me to lead, unaffected by the changing world around me and anchored by something true, real, and lasting.

Life Lesson #19. Be honest and seek truth.

In a recent study, it was discovered that 80% of parents lie to their kids...on a regular basis! Some fibs seem as banal as telling kids something will happen to them if they don't eat their veggies; others as dramatic and disturbing as lying about their past or their family. Kids, not surprisingly, model what they witness at home, and lying is no exception. Wavering standards for truthfulness within the family are dangerous in that they form a tapestry of deceit.

It's important to be as truthful as possible with your kids. Obviously some information might need to be shared later in their lives or shared at another time or place, but ultimately truth needs to win out in the home. If we can't be honest with those that love us most, who can we be ourselves with?

Our kids will also be influenced by less than truthful sources at school, with friends, and through the images they encounter. They need to build a grid so that they can recognize truthfulness when they hear it and learn to be truthful and full of integrity themselves.

When we seek God and God's will, we can, in turn, teach our children about life with values and truths they can rely on. They can anchor themselves to a moral and ethical framework that will lead them, center them, protect them, and guide them in every situation throughout their lives.

In a world lacking moral direction, our children are seeking to be led and taught integrity and truth.

They will be pulled toward the strongest influences they encounter. Let the greatest influence be you. Allow your own life to be calibrated by God, and then the differences you desire to see in this world will begin with you and your family.

Don't wait to commit to a relationship with God—start now.

I remember weeks after we had our son, we were home having breakfast while reading the paper. My husband seemed more engrossed than usual in articles on every page. I commented that it was a terribly interesting issue and that lately the news had seemed to be more compelling. I'll never forget my husband's response.

He said it felt as if his eyes had been opened. Now that we had a child, what was happening in the world seemed to take on a whole new significance. Suddenly things interested him that didn't before. He now saw and cared about things he hadn't before.

We looked at each other and knew that that would likely hold true for the rest of our lives. As single people and then as a young, married couple without children, we saw things through a telescope. We certainly looked down the lens of life seeing things more vividly than we had before. But as parents, we now saw things through a kaleidoscope. The colors were more complex, constantly changing, with a transparent beauty; we were not seeing just one piece but many playing in concert with each other. Life wasn't just more vivid; it was more interconnected. Our moment at the breakfast table showed us how differently we saw things because our perspective and experience had changed.

And so it is with God. We often see God as this big distant being outside our daily lives but He is, in fact, the very light behind the kaleidoscope waiting to show us the color, shape, and beauty of life, looking to guide us, hear us, and know us—the very friend we've always longed for.

One of the most important decisions of your life has to do with what kind of role you will take in regard to your family. But I am convinced that the most important decision you will ever make is where you are in regard to your faith. It is faith that allows you the perspective and wisdom that life and parenting require.

"For it is by grace you have been saved, through faith—
and this not from yourselves, it is the gift of God."
Ephesians 2:8

God might be speaking to your heart right now; don't hesitate to listen or to talk back. If you seek forgiveness for past mistakes or for choices you've made or feel like you continue to struggle with, He is ready to talk about it. If you seek love and grace in what feels like an impersonal and self-centered world, there is someone offering that love and grace to you in a selfless and gentle way. If you sense that something is missing in your life but you just can't put your finger on it, it is God knocking on the door of your heart, just wanting to have a conversation. He has promised to be with us always…even to the end of time.

And so I encourage you to step boldly into the life you've been specifically designed for, a life no one else can live, a life no one else can dare to dream.

It might seem overwhelming and daunting, but the biggest journey is started with the smallest step. Perhaps a start could be considering what leaving your job would look like, financially, personally, and physically, what your options might be, and what your methods would look. Perhaps it means sitting down with your spouse and discussing that your family could, in fact, dare to be counter-cultural, that every child in your family is too precious, too irreplaceable, and too valuable not to be made your highest priority.

Flying Blind

My best friend from college is a commercial airline pilot. When we were both still students, I flew with him once in a small two-seater Cessna over our college town. I still remember being amazed by the extraordinary caution he took before he ever dared to put that plane in the air. I expected safety. I trusted his judgment and experience, since he had grown up flying with a father who was a flight safety instructor. But I didn't expect the hour it took to painstakingly go through the pre-flight checklist. I think we spent more time preparing for the flight than we did in the air actually flying.

I think we too often jump into the captain's seat of parenting without really thinking about all the things that are a part of our journey. We are responsible for our kids, like passengers on our plane and who are at our mercy, at least for the first few years. They are unable to bail out if the flight gets bumpy or if the direction is unclear. But do we really think through the checklist of what parenting would and should look like? Or do we leave it up to chance, circumstance, or convenience? Do we have a flight plan? Or are we letting the winds of contemporary culture guide us? Did we intend to go one place and end up in another?

If we direct our families as if they were airplanes on course to a certain destination and commit to the plan and purpose of parenting, although things might threaten to throw us off course, we will be able to stand unwavering in our commitment to follow through. We can turn the tide of indifference, lack of involvement and spirituality, and the unguided moral direction that have become such a part of our culture today. But we must start at the grassroots level of our own homes.

The view from my ladder will be different from yours. At one point in my life, I knew I personally had to make a decision: did I really want to make my family a higher priority than my career? Because if I did, it meant I would have to make some tough choices. It would mean changing my focus and realigning my plans. It would ultimately mean leaping off my ladder and repositioning it on another wall.

I can only write from my experience, but from where I stand now, the sacrifice, commitment, and energy are slight compared with the joy of being able to see my son grow up right before my eyes. He knows by my actions that he is irreplaceable to me, and I know that no job, money, or creature comfort can begin to love me, enrich me, or bring me the happiness he does. I wouldn't trade a moment with him for anything in this world.

I don't want *any* parent to miss it.

Sometimes I fear we keep the things that are most important to us at arm's length. We hold God back with one arm and our most precious human relationships with another. Standing there with everything at bay we feel safe, strong, and in control. But we are meant to love and be loved, to know and be known, and to care and be cared for.

We need God and we need each other.

I knew that if I wished to encounter all that life has for me, I couldn't do it by keeping God or my family at arm's length. I had to take a step—just one small step—onto the carefully placed ladder of my family and climb slowly and deliberately toward a magnificent view.

I am hoping you will join me. It all begins with taking that first step.

Life Lesson #20. Fear need not rule the day.

The last life lesson I want to teach my son is to not be sidelined by fear. We all have fears in varying degrees about various things. Some fear death, some fear life, and perpetuating fear is certainly mainstream in our culture. One day I recognized that I could be fearful from dawn to dusk if I allowed myself to be.

For example: wake up, fear that my caffeine will be linked to cancer, my cereal is too sugary and will lead to diabetes, dust mites from my bed will fill my lungs, and the free radicals will have done an aging job on my face while I slept. I haven't even gotten out of my jammies yet.

Exercise thirty minutes a day or be overweight and have heart disease, drive slowly or get in an accident, don't text and drive, don't call and drive, don't drink and drive, don't eat red meat, don't eat dairy, don't eat high fructose corn syrup or MSG. Put antibacterial gel on hands a hundred times a day, and for heaven's sake, never touch a public phone, bathroom doorknob, shopping cart, or hotel bedspread. Pesticides are killing us, the air is choking us, the environment is warming, the hormones are changing us, the pharmaceuticals are weakening us, our food is supersizing us.

What are people living in the new millennium to do? We could be frightened of everything, everywhere, all the time.

Afraid to step on a plane, afraid to break an old habit, fearful of commitment, scared to death of what we can't control. It can paralyze us, deter us, and distract us.

I want my son to live a life as free of fear as possible. Fearlessness in this regard is not to be mistaken for foolishness or reckless abandon. Certainly some things in life require caution and reason. But living in fear is good for no one and accomplishes nothing. Hopefully we learn that we can't control what we weren't in control of in the first place. It just takes some of us longer than others to figure that out.

Trusting God for the outcomes in life and relying on Him to see you through the difficulties and trials are key.

I can't keep bad things from happening to me or my family. I can be preemptive, cautious, and guarded, but it will not mean a life free of trouble or pain. I can let fear dominate my life and dictate all that I do, or I can live life fully and freely, knowing that God is in control and has His hand in everything. I choose to live the latter.

I choose God's plan for my life over what is offered in glossy magazines or on the television. I choose God's plan for my life over what the world says my plan should be. I choose God's plan for my life over what I think it should be, because ultimately it's more interesting, fun, and fulfilling.

I choose God's plan for my marriage, my parenting, my view of success, and my identity. And regardless of how my life plays out, I know that the story was uniquely mine and specifically authored by the God who created me and knows me.

I don't fear that I'm not the parent I should be because I have a plan toward being the parent I can be. I don't fear that my identity is threatened by claiming motherhood as a profession because I've found such joy in where I am today. I don't fear what the media or the culture tells me to fear because I am confident in the impact I can make today, the direction our family is heading, and the priorities we've chosen.

For me, parenting full time was the right choice. It was a journey to get here and I'm not fully there yet. The desire of my heart no longer involves promotions or prestige. It involves knowing I have my priorities straight and my motives in line.

So, regardless of what decisions you make about your own parenting or whether or not you should work outside the home, I am hoping you seek to set the priorities in your life, particularly when it comes to your family. And ultimately I pray you choose to seek God and His plan for your life.

If you are right now wondering how to begin a relationship with God, it can be as easy as starting with this prayer:

Lord Jesus,
Come into my heart.
Change me, help me,
Forgive me.
Guide me closer to you.
Give me wisdom and
Help me discern your voice.
I want to know you.
Help me start living
In you
Today.

Be with me
In my decision
To stay home for my family
Or not.
Help me to know your will.
Give me the courage
To respond to your call
And the ability to do it.
Be with our family.
Be in the center of our lives.
Help me be brave enough
To start
Today.

Amen.

"For God so loved the world that he gave his one and only Son, that whoever believes in him shall not perish but have eternal life. For God did not send his Son into the world to condemn the world, but to save the world through him."
~ John 3:16–17

20 Life Lessons to Teach Our Own Children

Life Lesson #1.   Our work is not who we are.

Life Lesson #2.   How to handle adversity.

Life Lesson #3.   A parent's love is unconditional.

Life Lesson #4.   It is crucial to be spiritually grounded.

Life Lesson #5.   How to make tough moral choices.

Life Lesson #6.   Seek to find balance in life.

Life Lesson #7.   The value of hard work and discipline.

Life Lesson #8.   The true value of money.

Life Lesson #9.   How to be a good friend.

Life Lesson #10.   Don't be afraid to be your own person. Leaders often stand alone.

Life Lesson #11.   Being independent is good; being interdependent is better.

Life Lesson #12.   Guard your heart and mind.

Life Lesson #13.   Take care of yourself.

Life Lesson #14.   The blessing of a grateful spirit.

Life Lesson #15.   Find value in our individual contribution to others.

Life Lesson #16.   Strive for excellence and never stop learning.

Life Lesson #17.   Cherish the moment you're in.

Life Lesson #18.   Love is a commitment.

Life Lesson #19.   Be honest and seek truth.

Life Lesson #20.   Fear need not rule the day.

Dedication

I want to thank those who contributed in their own ways to the making of this book.

To my husband and best friend, Ken, who is a daily inspiration. You've helped make another dream come true. I love you. You're amazing.

To my son, Kasey, who made me a mom, and has made me glad to be one every single day. I love you more than you will ever know.

To my friends at Nelson Publishing & Marketing, your vision and your faith in this book made it a reality. Thank you for seeing what I couldn't.

To my dear friends and professors, Dr. Eugene Mayhew, Dr. Bruce Fong, and Dr. John Jelinek, who guided me, taught me, and believed in me, I thank you.

To my parents, Jonah and Pluma, God had it planned I would be yours. I wish I could thank you in person for your love and contribution to my life. I hope to someday.

And to my Lord and Savior, Jesus Christ, I thank you for your grace, your unfailing love, the vision you gave me, and the ability to write it. These are your words. I hope I didn't get in your way.

"May the words of my mouth and the meditation of my heart be pleasing in your sight, O Lord, my Rock and my Redeemer."
~ Psalm 19:14

Photo by Mark Steele from marksteelephotography.com

After more than ten years in the broadcast television industry, Sandy Calwell stepped out of the job arena to stay home and raise her son, Kasey. She gradually realized that many of the same skills and techniques she relied on in the working world were transferable to her new role. She also learned the importance of staying grounded, focused, and motivated as a parent.

Sandy was born in Wichita, Kansas. She currently lives in central Ohio with her husband, Ken, and son, Kasey. Sandy stays extremely active by running, biking, and playing tennis and golf. She also enjoys reading and cooking.

Sandy holds a BA in Journalism and an MA in Christian Education. This is her first book.